PRACTICAL | COMMON-SENSE | HISTORICALLY-SUPPORTED

Christianity
in a Doubting Age

Norman B. Smith

BOOK DESIGN BY: Catherine Smith Clegg

EDITED BY: Wayne Parris

EDITORIAL ASSISTANCE BY: Kevin Uppercue

Illustrations, unless otherwise identified, are from the *Bibbia Borso d'Este,* the most beautifully
and sumptuously illuminated Bible ever produced. Commissioned by the Marchese of Ferrera, it
was begun in 1455 and completed in 1461. The illuminations are by the painters Taddeo Crivelli
and Franco dei Russi. The *Bibbia* is now in the Estense Library in Modena, Italy.

TITLE: *Practical, Common-Sense, Historical
Christianity in a Doubting Age,* paper
ISBN 978-0-87775-961-4

PUBLISHER:
Alan Brilliant

Table of CONTENTS

Works of Art

${\mathcal A}$CKNOWLEDGEMENTS

${\mathcal M}$Y ELDEST DAUGHTER CATHERINE, who designed this book, a gardener and a herder of sheep, and whose daughters Alexa (age 9) and Sarah (age 7), created the art pieces, *Israelite Hut in Egypt at the Passover* and *Anasazi Flood Story*. My son Julian, who designed and posted this book's web site, fellow Missouri Synod Lutheran, Army Green Beret, Triathlon, Ironman, and Leadman, who climbs sheer rock faces in summer and frozen waterfalls in winter; who worked out with me a number of themes of this book in our weekly Sunday telephone calls, including the relationship of the Council of Nicea to Biblical inerrancy. My middle daughter Palmer, Peace Corps volunteer to Mauritania (in West Africa, one of the poorest countries in the world), herder of cattle, wife and mother of trout fishermen, and witness to the small miracle at the holy well. My youngest daughter Alexa, archaeologist of the Anasazi and other southwestern cultures, mother of Maisie ("child of light"), and witness to the small miracle at the holy well. My editor Wayne, humanist and scholar of Western civilization, fellow parishioner at Ebenezer Lutheran Church, who edited with a light hand and a generous heart. My publisher Alan, proprietor of Unicorn Press and Glenwood Community Bookshop, the best book man I have known (and I have known many). My editorial assistant Kevin, person of many talents, who greatly improved the text with a *Chicago Style Manual* in one hand and a sharp scalpel in the other. Molly, retired Presbyterian minister, who tediously but cheerfully checked and vetted all the Biblical references. Henry, art history student, who selected, annotated, and arranged the 63 works of art in the appendix. My valued and trusted secretary Bonnie, a faithful and devout Jehovah's Witness, who uncomplainingly and expertly typed and retyped the manuscript in change after change. Courtney, my able assistant, who unfailingly found facts, whether about tall buildings or bloodless revolutions, and tediously prepared the original indices. Carolyn, my beloved wife, who has been encouraging and supportive of this venture, and whose concepts and suggestions were instrumental in Chapter Ten, Holy Trinity, which most people think is the best chapter in the book.

PREFACE

THIS IS AN AGE of information, misinformation, and disinformation. We are bombarded with facts, theories, philosophies — on the bookshelf, at the newsstand, and over the internet in such quantities that we cannot hope to read them, much less make sense of them. Never before in history has so much unreasoned and unedited information been made available to us. If ever we needed our common sense and our reason, it is now. We need our common sense and our reason to separate the wheat from the chaff, the good from the bad, the sensible from the senseless.

Christianity has taken some hard hits in this tough environment. Snap judgments are made based on a lack of correct information. We fall too easily into analytical frameworks that are not rationally sustainable.

Christianity is fully justifiable and supportable under the most rigorous intellectual analysis. Indeed, the deeper and more thoughtful the reasoned analysis, the more Christianity is vindicated as the very best, worthiest belief system that is or can be. It seems to me that Peter Abelard (he who had the fateful forbidden love affair with Heloise), who depended on human reason to justify Christianity, had the better side of the argument with Saint Bernard, who regarded faith as the sole support of the Christian religion.

In these pages I attempt to connect the dots, so to speak, in support of Christianity, by drawing together and considering rational, theological, historical, and practical information from diverse sources.

DEDICATION

TO GABRIELLA PALMER WILSON SMITH, my wife for 42 years until she was called by God to join Him in heaven, a victim of cancer. She died at dawn on All Saints Day, November 1, 2004. And a saint she was. She bore our four children and raised them without nearly as much help from me as there should have been. They are all fine, wonderful people, and there are seven grandchildren, five of whom my wife lived long enough to see. Gay did not live to see Maisie, whose name means "child of light", or her namesake Gabriella, the seventh of that name in straight succession from the niece of Sir Francis Drake. From the time we married until two years before Gay's death, I was a Unitarian; she was a lifelong Episcopalian. When I would not say the creed or take communion on account of my religious scruples, she was never critical or impatient. All of our children were christened and confirmed in the Episcopal Church.

TO JOSHUA HAUGEN, my pastor at Ebenezer Lutheran (Missouri Synod) Church in Greensboro, North Carolina. After a chaotic, but mercifully brief, second marriage ended, it was necessary for me to change churches. I attended a service at Ebenezer. I witnessed the devotion, enthusiasm, and good humored spirit of the members of Ebenezer, and I knew right away that this was the church for me. Joshua very kindly and gently guided me through instruction, a prerequisite to membership. When he made it clear that Biblical inerrancy is a basic belief of Missouri Synod Lutherans, I thought I might have a problem, but soon found that total belief in the Bible is far easier and far more satisfying than the selective belief of the Bible that is the standard in mainline Protestant denominations today. I rarely miss one of Joshua's Sunday morning and Wednesday evening Bible studies. He has a near-perfect memory, amazing analytical abilities, and above all, deep Christian faith. He is fluent in Greek and Hebrew, and is knowledgeable in church history, relevant archaeological discoveries, and the major theologians. For most of the thoughts in this book, I am indebted to Joshua's teaching and discussions in his class, although he mildly expresses disagreement on several points where I depart from established Lutheran doctrines.

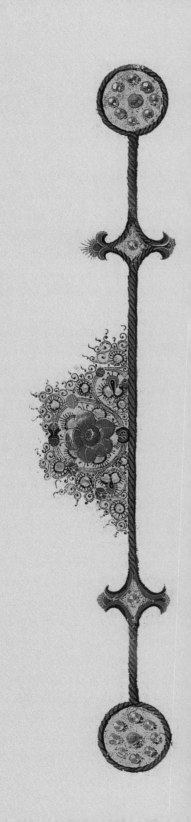

INTRODUCTION

My FATHER HAD BEEN a Baptist, and my mother was a Methodist, but neither was a churchgoer, until Mother developed cancer when I was a teenager, and then she and I began attending a Methodist church with some regularity. In my senior year of high school, I developed an interest in Unitarianism.

Early in my freshman year at the University of North Carolina in Chapel Hill, I began attending services at a non-denominational church that was Unitarian in all but name. From that point and for the next forty-five years or so, I regarded myself to be a Unitarian, from time to time attending services and enrolling as a member at our Unitarian church in Greensboro. Over the years I began to drift to the more theologically conservative side of Unitarianism, thinking of myself as a Christian Unitarian.

Then three momentous events occurred in my life. The first involved a stubborn, very itchy, somewhat painful, and ever expanding fungus infection on both of my feet, a condition that had persisted for thirty years. Dermatologists had treated the condition, always to no avail. In the spring of 1991, my wife, my daughters Palmer and Alexa, and I were touring Wales. For some reason we became interested in healing wells of which there are scores in Wales, originally connected with the Druidic religion, but later absorbed by the Christian church. We were at Saint Gybi's well near the Llangybi Church in the north of Wales. It was a glorious spring morning. Wallflowers and primroses were abundant in the fresh green meadow. Baby lambs were all around us. The well, long fallen into neglect and disuse, was formed by a crystalline spring that flowed out of a rocky formation. On the sides of the pool, we could see remnants of an ancient stone chapel — the remains of walls, seats, a baptismal font. Purely as a lark and without a shred of religiosity, I took off my shoes and socks and dabbled my feet in the water for a few minutes. On the way back to the car I could feel the lesions healing, and within three days, not only were the lesions gone, but my natural skin was restored clean and unscarred. No possible natural phenomena could account for the healing. I had been the recipient of a small miracle, but why I was healed of a relatively trivial condition I will never understand, when there are so many uncured cases of paralysis, blindness, insanity, cancer, heart failure, and other major afflictions. Even though I had been healed, I still did not become a Christian.

A year or so later, my wife and I were in Florence, Italy, at the Convento di San Marco. This monastery is filled with frescos and paintings by Fra Angelico. We were turning a corner, preparing to walk upstairs to tour the monks' cells, when I was stopped in my tracks by a magnificent, luminous, vibrant Fra Angelico fresco of the Annunciation. There it was in all its glory, bathed in the gentle Italian spring morning sunshine. The Blessed Virgin was amazingly beautiful, demure but strong, and the Archangel Gabriel had his delicate, feathery, outspread and intensely colorful wings. I said to myself at that moment, "You know, the angel did come to Mary to tell her that she would conceive by the Holy Spirit and give birth to the Son of God." Yet I still did not become a Christian.

A year or two after that my wife, my daughter Catherine, and I were at the Prado in Madrid. We had been upstairs to see five rooms of paintings by Velasquez and had toured the first floor where there were immense canvases by De Goya, Murillo, and Zuburan. I was descending stairs to the basement to see some smaller sized works of the Northern Renaissance, when I turned a corner and there I was face to face with Rogier Van der Weyden's *Descent from the Cross:* Christ's body being lovingly and tenderly removed from the cross by Joseph of Aramathea and Nichodemus in the presence of a fainting Blessed Virgin, Saint John the Evangelist, Saint Mary Magdalene, the other Saint Mary, and Saint Martha. This is an amazing, beautifully executed, captivating painting. I said to myself, "You know, that really happened. Jesus really did suffer and die for us on the cross to gain remission of our sins and to give us the promise of everlasting life." I did not become a Christian right away, but soon afterwards I did.

The miraculous cure, the Annunciation, and the *Descent from the Cross,* ultimately overwhelmed me. I converted to Christianity. I was baptized in a small Methodist church in the Appalachian mountains on a cold winter's day, and immediately began reciting the creed and taking communion in good conscience.

I am descended from Clovis I, a fifth century King of Cologne.* He was converted to Christianity and baptized late in that century. Until recently, I thought in Gibbonian terms that Clovis was of the barbaric hordes that destroyed Roman civilization, and who must have been living in an uncivilized state and worshiping all sorts of primitive gods found in rivers and trees. Recent scholarship now informs me that Clovis most likely was an educated and intelligent man who had served as an officer in the Roman army, and like many of the Roman army officers of the time, had embraced the Arian heresy, a primitive sort of Unitarianism, until his Christian conversion. It is startling to learn that my ancestor Clovis converted from a sort of Unitarianism to Christianity, just as I did fifteen hundred years later.

All Biblical quotations in the book are from the English Standard Version.

* Clovis I *(King of Cologne)*
  Clovis the Riparian *(King of Cologne)*
  Childebert *(King of Cologne)*
  Siegbert the Lame *(King of Cologne)*
  Cloderic the Parricide *(King of Cologne)*
  Munderic of Vitry-en-Perthois
  Bodegisel I
  Bodegisel II
  Saint Arnulf
  Duke Ansgise
  Pepin of Heristal
  Charles Martel *(defeated Muslims at Tours in 733)*
  Pepin the Short *(Frankish King)*
  The Emperor Charlemagne
  Louis the Fair *(Holy Roman Emperor)*
  Charles the Bald *(King of France)*
  Louis II the Stammerer *(King of France)*
  Charles III the Simple *(King of France)*
  Louis IV D'Outre-Mere *(King of France)*
  Charles *(Duke of Lorraine)*
  Gerberga *(wife of Lambert I, Count of Louvain)*
  Maud of Louvain
  Lambert of Boulogne *(companion of William the Conqueror at Battle of Hastings)*
  Judith of Lens *(niece of William the Conqueror)*
  Maud of Huntingdon *(married to Simon of St. Liz, Crusader, and then to Scottish King David I)*

Maud St. Liz
Walter Fitz Robert
Robert Fitz Walter *(leader of the Barons who forced King John to sign the Magna Carta)*
Sir Walter Fitz Robert
Ella Fitz Walter
Margaret de Odyngsells
Sir John De Grey *(Baron of Rotherfield)*
Maud De Grey
Sir Thomas de Harcourt
Sir Richard Harcourt
Ellis Harcourt
Elizabeth Bessiles
Anne Fettiplace
Mary Purefoy
Susanna Thorne
Thomas Dudley *(Governor of Massachusetts Bay Colony)*
Deborah Dudley
Deborah Wade
David Dunster
Mary Dunster
John Bemis *(soldier in
    the American Revolution)*
Abigail Bemis
Arozina Hildreth
Sidney Hildreth Barrett
Mabel Eva Barrett
Donald Barrett Smith
Norman Barrett Smith

Baptism of Clovis I (496 AD)
Stained glass window.
BAPTISTRY, COLLEGIATE CHURCH OF NOTRE-DAME,
POISSY, FRANCE.

Chapter One
CAIN *and* ABEL

C AIN WAS A TILLER OF THE SOIL, a grower of arable crops. Abel was a herdsman, a keeper of sheep. Cain offered of his grains and fruits to God, but God was not pleased with the offering. Abel sacrificed one of his lambs to God, and God was pleased. Cain was so incensed by God's acceptance of his brother's gifts, and God's rejection of his own gifts, that he killed his brother. Then he compounded his crime by denying to God knowledge of what he had done asking, "Am I my brother's keeper?" *(Genesis 4:1-9)*.

It seems counter intuitive that fruits of the earth would be rejected by God, while a bloody and burned lamb should be acceptable in His sight. The solution to this paradox may lie in the differentiated patterns of practice of crop-growing societies from herding cultures, going to the dawn of recorded history both in the Old and New Worlds. Cultures that tilled the soil universally tended to be autocratic, authoritarian, and hierarchical; whereas herding societies tended to be relatively flexible and even democratic in a primitive way. See, for example, the account of Korah's rebellion in *Numbers 16:3:* "For all in the congregation are holy, every one of them .... Why then do you exalt yourselves above the assembly of the Lord?" Worst of all, ancient arable farming cultures regularly practiced the ultimate form of inhumanity: ritual human sacrifice.

Thus, we can perceive God's plan for his faith best to grow and prosper in a society of herders, where relative human freedom prevailed and at least the seeds of democracy were present. Remember how God throughout the historical parts of the Old Testament continually reminds the Israelites (nomadic people and traditional herders) that they must not worship Molech and Ba'al, gods of crop cultures that required human sacrifice. See, for example, *Numbers 25:2-5,* and *Psalms 37* and *106.*

Cain, true to the inclination of ancient arable farming cultures, carried out human sacrifice, even of his own brother. Since Jesus in the Gospels most often referred to Himself as the Son of Man (79 times in the Gospels), his manifestation, as not only the savior of men and women, but also our brother, must be recognized. In Abel's death, thus, we have a forecast of Jesus' own death, at the hands of His brothers, our ancestors — the high priests, the Pharisees, Pilate and his government, and the mob who demanded His death.

Abel had sacrificed a lamb, and this led inexorably to his own death. The lamb was made to bleed, and undoubtedly the blood fell on the wood, the fuel of the altar fire. The sacrifices, both by and of Abel, occurring very early in the Old Testament, point to the sacrifice of Jesus in the New Testament. Jesus is called the Lamb of God in the *Gospel of John (1:29, 36)*. Yet he is also referred to as the Good Shepherd *(John 10:11, 12, 14)*.

Proto-democratic tendencies are found in the ancient herding cultures. Is it possible to make a case for democracy being a form of government, especially when it has been peaceably attained, that is particularly favored and blessed by the Almighty? Perhaps the tracing of the thread begins with the account of the fall of Jericho's walls in the Sixth Chapter of Joshua. The Israelites are instructed by God to march around the city for seven days, with seven priests bearing seven trumpets of rams' horns before the Ark of the Covenant; on the seventh day they are to march around Jericho seven times, and on the last circuit when a long blast is sounded on the trumpets, the people shall shout "with a great shout, and the wall of the city will fall down flat ...." This exactly took place, and Jericho was conquered without a single arrow being shot, without a single spear being thrust. Consider the following bloodless revolutions in the course of recent human history, which, with essential contributions by Christians, established democracies:

ℛ On April 17, 1688, King James II of England commanded the clergy to read a declaration at divine services that was contrary to acts of Parliament. Seven bishops drew up a petition to the king protesting this order in the humblest terms. The king prosecuted the seven bishops for seditious libel. The jury refused to convict the bishops even though the evidence of their having signed and presented the petition was uncontradicted. The king discovered that the clergy throughout the realm had refused to read the declaration. He appealed to the army to enforce his mandate. He told the first regiment, good Christians all, that those who did not think fit to subscribe to the royal order should lay down their arms, and nearly all did. On November 6, 1688, King James II fled in a boat across the Thames and into exile. The Prince of Orange invaded with no armed resistance. Not a shot was fired. Great Britain has remained a democratic constitutional monarchy to this day.

In 1981 an alliance of powerful military officers had plotted a coup to overthrow Spain's new democratic government. Following the death of the dictator Franco in 1975, Spain had peacefully adopted reforms supported by nearly ninety percent of the voters in national referenda, establishing a parliamentary democracy and guaranteeing equality before the law and a full range of individual liberties including freedom of religion. Spanish monarchs for centuries had looked upon themselves as the most Christian and Catholic of all rulers. King Juan Carlos walked on February 23, 1981, at the head of an immense popular march, supporting the democratic reforms, putting his own life on the line. The disloyal military commanders were overwhelmed and gave up. Not a shot was fired. Democratic government has continued in Spain to this day without interruption.

In January, 1986, a dishonest election was held in the Republic of the Philippines. By virtue of force and fraud, henchmen of the cruel and rapacious dictator Ferdinand Marcos declared him to be victorious. Jaime Sin, a recently appointed cardinal, led the popular resistance to the continuation of Marcos's rule. Massive political rallies opposing Marcos sprung up. Radio Veritas, the Catholic radio station, acted as the voice of the popular revolt. Evangelical Protestants stood shoulder to shoulder with the Catholic protestors. Reminiscent of the taking of Jericho long ago, the Christians sang hymns, prayed, and read the Bible. The secretary of defense of the republic announced his alignment with the popular resistance. The perimeters of the defense department were lightly defended by soldiers loyal to the secretary. Marcos ordered an attack on the defense department by a tank regiment of marines believed to be loyal to him. As the head tank was ordered to drive forward into the ranks of kneeling priests and nuns, all ready to sacrifice their lives, the marines refused to move. Two days later in early February, 1986, Marcos fled the country. Not a shot was fired. Democracy was re-established in the Philippines, where it has thrived ever since.

In 1989, the Soviet Union and puppet states of Eastern Europe began the process of disintegration. This development is directly traceable to Catholic resistance to communism in Poland, where the people built churches in defiance of the authorities, carried crucifixes in pro-democratic public parades and gatherings, and even successfully obtained a visit from Pope John Paul II. It is not widely known, but true, that both Mikhail Gorbachev and Boris Yeltsin, the last general secretaries of the Soviet communist party, when infants, were taken by their mothers for baptism in Russian Orthodox churches. These men led Russia in a bloodless revolution in which communist dictatorship ended and for the most part, democratic governments were established in Russia, along with the other fifteen republics of the Soviet Union, and Poland, East Germany, Czechoslovakia, Hungary, Romania, Bulgaria, Yugoslavia, and Albania. Perhaps the most dramatic event of the fall of communism was the entirely peaceful dismantling of the Berlin Wall in November, 1989, accompanied by shouts and the blare of musical instruments, just as the wall of ancient Jericho had come tumbling down.

On February 11, 2011, a huge popular and peaceful uprising in Egypt, which lasted less than three weeks, resulted in Hosni Mubarak, a dictator for thirty years, resigning and dismantling his government. He, his family, and his friends had systematically looted this impoverished country. Mubarak's regime had regularly employed torture, imprisonment without trial, and extrajudicial execution. They had denied voting rights and systematically suppressed speech, petition, and assembly. The army refused the orders of Mubarak to move against the demonstrators. In a nation of eighty million, the most populous Arab country, less than eight hundred and fifty lost their lives. Under a caretaker military government, early elections and the adoption of a democratic constitution are promised. While the ideology of the pro-democracy protestors was largely secular, there was wide participation in the movement by Coptic Christians, a substantial minority in Egypt. The triggering event of the popular unrest may have been the bombing of a Coptic church in Alexandria, resulting in widespread Christian protests, not against Muslims, but against the government. These protests grew more intense after a Copt was shot by a policeman on January 14, and within ten days the generalized uprising began in which Muslims, Christians, and secularists all participated.

∾ Would the events in 1989 at Tiananmen Square in the People's Republic of China, have ended with the adoption of a democratic government, had there been substantial Christian participation in the popular uprising or the army units that were called in to suppress it? Shots were fired, people were crushed by tanks, and the communist dictatorship was preserved.

The Cain and Abel story is the first precursor of the Crucifixion found in the Old Testament. The next of these precursors is the Abraham-Isaac story. Abraham was ordered by God to sacrifice his own son *(Genesis 22:1-14)*. Abraham was preparing to carry out the order when a ram appeared, and with God's approval, was made the substitute offering. Abraham's servants had carried wood to the offering site (which was actually where the Temple was later erected). Isaac's blood would have flowed, and the blood of the ram did flow, on the wood which was to be consumed in the altar fire. God thus spared Abraham's son Isaac, just as He was to spare the firstborn sons of Israel in the Passover, just as he has spared, preserved, and nurtured to maturity so many of us, all children of Abraham as we are. Yet He sacrificed His own dear blessed Son, whose precious blood flowed upon the wooden cross, so that we, our ancestors, and our descendants, should have our sins forgiven and have eternal life only by believing in Him.

Chapter Two
The BIBLE

ARTIN LUTHER AND JOHANNES GUTENBERG brought the Bible out of the exclusive possession of the clergy into the hands of all the people. Luther, who translated the Bible from Latin to the vernacular, believed that every Christian should be able to possess and study the Bible and stream its messages into his own life. Gutenberg's printing press, which published the Bible first and foremost, produced the Bible in sufficient quantities and at costs for them to be widely available to laity and clergy alike. The Bible remains the best-selling book in all times and in all seasons. Even today, worthy organizations like the Gideons and the Lutheran Laymen's League labor to make Bibles available everywhere to everybody, including especially nations recently emerging from communism where Bibles were systematically suppressed for decades.

When I took courses in the Old and New Testaments from a distinguished professor of religion at the University of North Carolina in Chapel Hill in the late 1950s, I was instructed that we had to believe in the truth of the New Testament, but that the Old Testament was nothing but myth and metaphor. It did not take me long to conclude reasonably that if the Old Testament were false, the New Testament likewise must be false. My gravitation toward Unitarianism became irresistible, and there I remained for forty-five years or so.

The professor was wrong. To begin with, merely because a reported event is symbolic or metaphoric does not mean that it did not occur. It means only that the event had such resonance and that memory of it was so well preserved, that it became significant in other contexts and to explain other phenomena. To illustrate this proposition in a non-religious context, consider the event of the attack on Pearl Harbor on December 7, 1941. The event is often referred to metaphorically, as in the expression "We have Pearl Harbored you." Therefore, to acknowledge an historical event's metaphoric character, in no way undermines the truth of its occurrence.

Some of the reported events in the Old Testament have been debunked on the theory that they depart from the laws of nature. Yet the very quality of miracles is that God, the One who prescribed for the world the laws of nature, has chosen to depart from the natural order in a given instance for the purpose of carrying out His divine will. Rather than struggling to find some sort of wind or tidal occurrence to explain the parting of the Red Sea *(Exodus 14:15-31)*, it is sufficient, and indeed preferable, to regard it as an act of divine intervention.

Some of the recorded miracles have ancient records from diverse non-Jewish cultures to support them, as in the case of a widely observed aberration in the earth's rotation that coincides with the "sun standing still" at the Battle of Gibeon *(Joshua 10:12-14)*.

Certain Old Testament miracles also have to be evaluated in the context of Hebraic linguistic and expressive patterns. Hebrew is known for its using exaggerated statements to drive home a point, a concept that would have been clearly understood and allowed for by contemporary audiences, but not by us in the twenty-first century. When Samson killed one thousand Philistines with the jawbone of an ass *(Judges 15:14-16)*, the true facts well could have been that with his great strength and agility, Samson killed several Philistines with this very weapon, and thereby boosted the fighting spirit of his fellow warriors to such a degree that a total of one thousand Philistines were killed, all killed because Samson had used the jawbone of an ass as a lethal weapon.

Still other recorded miracles are difficult to fathom as a practical matter. For the life of me, I cannot figure out how two of each of all of the species were herded aboard Noah's Ark and were able to survive there for forty-plus days. But simply because Norman Smith is not wise enough to figure this out, it does not nullify that miracle, nor by extension, does it call into question the other miracles of the Bible. Before rejecting the flood story out of hand, pause to reflect for a moment that virtually every culture and every faith of the world recounts the event of the flood. Consider these lines from Ovid's *Metamorphoses (Book the First,* lines 287-296, 313-314, 319-322, 325-326):

> Th' expanded waters gather on the plain:
> They float the fields, and over-top the grain;
> Then rushing onwards, with a sweepy sway,
> Bear flocks, and folds, and lab'ring hinds away,
> Nor safe their dwellings were, for, sap'd by floods,
> Their houses fall upon their household Gods.

The solid piles, the strongly built to fall,
High o'er their heads, behold a watry wall:
Now seas and Earth were in confusion lost;
A world of waters, and without a coast.

A mountain of stupendous height there stands
Betwixt th' Athenian and Boetian lands,...
High on the summit of this dubious cliff,
Deucalion wafting, moor'd his little skiff.
He with his wife were only left behind
of perish'd man; they two were human kind....
The most upright of mortal men was he;
The most sincere, and holy woman, she.

Alexa Clegg (American, b. 2001).
Stylized Anasazi Great Flood Pictograph, 2011.
Watercolor on paper.
PRIVATE COLLECTION.

Not long after reading these lines, I visited the Anasazi cliff dwellings and rock art in Canyon De Chelly in Arizona. There I saw a pictograph, painted before Europeans, Asians, and Africans had any contact with the Western Hemisphere. It depicted a rather relieved looking man and woman, a rainbow, and a bird bearing a green branch.

A common argument against the truth of the Old Testament focuses on Adam and Eve. It is claimed that the Biblical account must be false because they could not have reproduced, given the uniform law and taboo against marriages within the nuclear family, a prohibition that tends to preserve the soundness of the human species, protecting it from all manner of birth defects. Before you accept this argument, take a closer look at the text of Genesis. On the sixth day or epoch of creation, "God created man in his own image, in the image of God he created him; male and female he created them. And God blessed them. And God said to them, 'Be fruitful and multiply and fill the earth…'" *(Genesis 1:27-28)*. On the seventh day or epoch, God rested. Only after this, does Genesis refer to the creation of Adam and Eve and their placement in the Garden of Eden *(Genesis 2:7-8, 18-23)*. The creation of humans in Chapter One of Genesis is referred to as the creation of man, but clearly the reference is to mankind, since the text uses the plural pronoun "them." When it comes to the creation of Adam and Eve, in Chapter Two of Genesis, only the singular pronouns are used. What I suggest occurred is that it took a presumably long period of time for mankind to evolve to the point of having sufficient intelligence and socialization, to be able to comprehend and worship God and to distinguish between good and evil. It was at that point that God, taking no chances, specifically created Adam and Eve. When it came time for their children to marry, there were ample members of the human race in existence who could be selected as spouses.*

None of the Old Testament miracles are random or unconnected. Scores of them lead inexorably to Jesus on the cross and even beyond. These connections are enormously rich in symbolism and imagery. Consider, for example, the first plague visited upon the Pharaoh, water turning into blood. Blood can provide some nourishment, but this blood putrefied and would provide no nourishment nor slake the thirst. It should be noted that only the surface waters were changed to blood; the aquifer was unaffected so that the Egyptians were able to obtain water by digging wells *(Exodus 7:20)*. The first miracle of Jesus was turning water into wine at the wedding feast in Cana of Galilee *(John 2:7-9)*. When a spear was thrust into Jesus' side while He hung on the cross, blood and water separately flowed out *(John 19:34)*. When He thirsted at the crucifixion, all that was given Him (to Him who had given the wedding guests the best of wine) was some vinegar, a liquid that does not relieve the thirst *(John 19:28-29)*. The miracle we of the traditional church experience every week at the Eucharist is wine being transformed into the blood of Christ. This completes the cycle from water to blood, water to wine, and wine back to blood. When the children of Israel, perhaps a million in number, wandered in the wilderness, God miraculously relieved their hunger by sending manna, the bread of heaven *(Exodus 16:14-32)*. The provision of bread, widely regarded to be the staff of life, is the subject of two of Jesus' miracles, the feeding of the thousands *(Matthew 14:15-21, 15:32-38; Mark 6:38-44, 8:5-9; Luke 9:13-17; John 6:9-13)*. At the weekly Eucharist, bread is miraculously transformed into the body of Christ, He who is called the bread of life *(John 6:35)*.

But let us turn directly to the Resurrection. This is the central miracle of the New Testament, the event on which the entire Christian faith hinges. The event is described essentially in identical detail by four Gospel writers, who worked independently and not in collaboration. It is true that the writers of the synoptic Gospels rely on other sources for information, but Saint John the Evangelist was there in person and saw that the stone had been removed from the tomb, and that the tomb was empty, and he saw with his own eyes the linen wrappings and the face cloth *(John 20:1-9)*. This same disciple John saw the resurrected Jesus on multiple occasions before he ascended to heaven forty days later *(John 20:19-22, 26; 21:20-22; Acts 1:3)*. As Saint John states in the penultimate paragraph of his Gospel, "This is the disciple who is bearing witness about these things, and who has written these things, and we know that his testimony is true" *(John 21:24)*. Also, it should be noted that Gospel writer Saint Matthew, who was a disciple of Jesus, whether or not he saw the empty tomb, had to have heard a number of first-person accounts of the events of the Resurrection. If this were not enough to prove beyond doubt the truth of Resurrection, we have yet another confirmation of the event. Flavius Josephus, a contemporary Jewish historian, who never converted to Christianity, also reports the occurrence of the Resurrection *(Antiquities, Volume II, Book XVIII)*.

This level of historical certainty and proof that supports the Resurrection of Christ is virtually unsurpassed in ancient history. We have fewer and less reliable sources for the details of the lives and deeds of Alexander the Great, Julius Caesar, Nebuchadnezzar, Alfred the Great, and Atilla the Hun, to name but a few of the great conquerors, yet there is essentially universal belief in the historical truth of their actions. These are but earthly kings whose kingdoms long ago disappeared. They were mere men, in the words of the Psalmist, whose "days are like grass; he flourishes like a flower of the field; for the wind passes over it and it is gone,..." *(Psalm 103:15-16).* But Christ is the Lord of Hosts, the King of Glory, the King of Kings, whose kingdom shall have no end *(Isaiah 44:6, John 18:36, 1 Timothy 6:14-15),* so there is even greater reason to have universal acceptance of the truth of the Resurrection of our Lord and Savior.

Another extremely valuable function of the Old Testament text that is often ignored is the unerring prediction of Christ's life, death, and resurrection. If you will, begin with the account of the Passover in which a lamb's blood is smeared on the lintels and doorposts of the huts of the children of Israel. Inside the dark interior, the precious firstborn are peacefully sleeping. The angel of the Lord kills all of the firstborn of the Egyptians, but spares those whose abodes are marked by the blood of the lamb. It does not take great imagination to realize that the right and left doorposts and the part of the

lintel pertaining to each, symbolically represent the T-shaped crosses on which the thieves were crucified, while within, where shadows preclude any apparition of the third cross, the sleeping firstborn who are protected by the blood of the lamb are metaphorically connected with the people of

Sarah Clegg (American, b. 2003). *Israelite Hut in Egypt at the Passover,* 2011. Tempura and pencil on paper. PRIVATE COLLECTION.

Christendom, whose lives, not just earthly lives but eternal lives are spared by Jesus, the Lamb of God, giving His own precious blood upon the cross for our salvation.

The relationship of Psalm 22 to the crucifixion of our Lord is clear and plain:

> I am...scorned by mankind and despised by the people.
> All who see me mock me; they make mouths at me; they wag their heads;...
> my strength is dried up like a potsherd and my tongue sticks to my jaws;...
> For dogs encompass me, a company of evildoers encircles me;
> they have pierced my hands and feet — ...
> they divide my garments among them, and for my clothing they cast lots.

It is noteworthy that crucifixion was not practiced or known at the time the Psalms were written down.

For a compelling prophecy of the life and ministry of our Lord, read *Isaiah 7:14, 9:6, 11:1-5:*

> Therefore, the lord himself will give you a sign. Behold, the virgin shall conceive and bear a son, and shall call his name Immanuel.

> There shall come forth a shoot from the stump of Jesse,
> And a branch from his roots shall bear fruit.

> For to us a child is born,
> to us a son is given;
> and the government shall be
> upon his shoulder,
> and his name shall be called
> Wonderful Counselor, Mighty God,
> Everlasting Father, Prince of Peace.

13

And the Spirit of the Lord shall rest upon him,
The Spirit of wisdom and understanding,
The Spirit of counsel and might,
The Spirit of knowledge and the fear of the Lord.
And his delight shall be in the fear of the Lord.
He shall not judge by what his eyes see, or decide disputes by what
    his ears hear,
But with righteousness he shall judge the poor,
And decide with equity for the meek of the earth;
And he shall strike the earth with the rod of his mouth,
And with the breath of his lips he shall kill the wicked.
Righteousness shall be the belt of his waist,
And faithfulness the belt of his loins.

Because these prophecies became fulfilled in precisely the way that was predicted, additional credence is given to the miracle of the Resurrection. From clearly fulfilled prophecies, it is important to distinguish numerous Biblical prophecies, often lacking precision, that seemingly have not been fulfilled. Simply because various leaders of certain denominations have proclaimed themselves empowered to interpret these prophecies, and the leaders invariably prove wrong when the prophetic date passes by without the predicted occurrence, this in no way undermines the truth of the prophecies of the Crucifixion and the Resurrection that have been fulfilled.

For even further proof of the Resurrection consider the relics, custody of which are maintained by the Catholic Church. Most Protestants bristle at the mere mention of relics. One of Martin Luther's earliest criticisms of the contemporary church, to be found in his lectures as a member of the theological faculty at Wittenburg long before he posted the *Ninety-five Theses,* was the church's proclamation and veneration of innumerable relics, many of which necessarily were counterfeit. He protested that if you put all of the pieces of the true cross together that were held by the church, you would have not just a cross, but a forest. Bishop Gilbert Burnet in *The History of the Reformation of the Church of England* (Vol. I, p. 242, 1681 edition) comments on the destruction of what he regarded to be false images and relics: "For their Images some of them were brought to London, and were there at St. Paul's Cross in the sight of all the People, broken; that they might be fully convinced of the jingling Impostures of the Monks."

Yet surely no rational person can conclude that simply because some or many of the relics were fakes, others were not genuine. I have no doubt that even today, fragments of the true cross are to be found in reliquaries maintained by the Catholic Church. A large part of the genuine relics were deliberately destroyed, either during the iconoclastic furies unleashed by the Protestant Reformation, especially in Calvinist lands, or during methodical destruction of religious artifacts by Muslims in Spain, Greece, the Middle East and North Africa; revolutionaries in France; and communists in Russia and Eastern Europe.**

Reliquary of the True Cross.
German (Swabia) before 1135. Gold, silver gilt over wood, enamel, gems.
KATHOLISCHES
MÜNSTERPFARRAMT,
Zwiefalten, Germany
(a portion of the true cross, together with a stone fragment from Christ's manger, a stone from Golgotha, a stone from the Holy Sepulcher, and a stone from the mountain of the Lord's Ascension).

15

When Christ was laid in the tomb, a shroud was placed over His face. This cloth was found in the empty tomb by Saint Peter, "not lying with the linen cloths but folded up in a place by itself" *(John 20:6-7).* It is claimed that this very cloth is the well-known Shroud of Turin, which still faintly bears Christ's apparent facial features. This artifact has been subjected to much scientific study and none of the studies rule out its genuineness.

As Jesus dragged the cross toward Golgotha, a woman stepped forward and wiped the blood and sweat from His face with her veil, and then the veil miraculously bore the image of Christ's bloody and sweaty face, according to ancient Catholic tradition. She is known as Saint Veronica. The name signifies True Image in Latin, clearly a pseudonym. It has been suggested that she was Saint Martha, sister of Lazarus. The association is meaningful since Jesus miraculously restored Lazarus to life after he had died *(John 11:14-15, 38-39, 43-44),* and Jesus was soon to die, be buried, and Himself arise from the dead. Simply because the Gospels fail to mention the incident of the veil does not mean it did not occur, for as Saint John the Evangelist tells us in the last paragraph of his Gospel, "Now there were also many other things

Rembrandt Van Rijn (Dutch, 1601–1669).
The Raising of Lazarus: the larger plate, c. 1632.
Copper plate etching and burin.
PLATE IN NORTH CAROLINA MUSEUM OF ART, RALEIGH.
On loan from the Park West Gallery and the Scaglione Family

that Jesus did. Were every one of these to be written, I suppose that the world itself could not contain the books that would be written." The cloth with the facial imprint of Jesus' image that the Catholic Church regards to be Veronica's veil, was left in the Vatican from the earliest times until about four hundred years ago when it went missing during renovations. The same year it disappeared from the Vatican, it showed up at a Capuchin monastery named Manoppello in the Apennines, where it has remained ever since. The facial shape and the characteristics of the hair on Veronica's veil are similar to those on the Shroud of Turin.

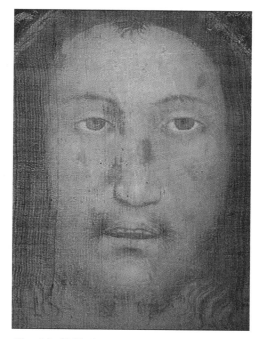

Veronica's Veil in its present state
BASILICA VOLTO SANTO DI MANOPPELLO, ITALY

No factual statement of either the Old Testament or the New Testament has been definitively proven by geological or archaeological evidence not to have occurred. What I propose is that there be a presumption of the truth of anything in the Bible, unless and until a part of it is conclusively proven to be false.

We hear occasionally of someone denying the occurrence of the Holocaust, the horrific destruction of Europe's Jews. Such deniers are uniformly regarded to be lunatics. There should be a clear presumption against denying the occurrence of any event that has the support of recorded history. Otherwise, we lose the great repository of our collective human experience from which numerous and invaluable lessons are learned that guide us to a more rational and morally superior future state. The philosopher Santayana said that to ignore history is to be condemned to repeat it.

According to the foregoing analysis, it makes much more sense to believe the Bible in its entirety, than selectively to doubt its truth, which leads ultimately to questioning and even rejecting the central tenet of Christianity, that

Jesus died to redeem us from our sins and to offer us the promise of eternal salvation. Once you have tried living with a trust in Biblical inerrancy for awhile, most assuredly you will become comfortable with it, and will have a far easier time navigating through life's trials and tribulations, than you would have with a self-selected mixture of partial truth and partial falsehood of the Bible. You will find that it is far easier and more comforting to ask how or why a certain Biblical statement is true, rather than whether or not it is false. In your analysis of reason to support Biblical truths, you will attain astonishingly and deeply satisfying new insights into scripture.

In Chapter 3 I suggest that the church was impoverished by its failure to deal positively with the products of new thinking in the social and physical sciences, including Copernican-Galilean astronomy, Darwinian evolution, Marxist communism, and Freudian psychology. You may wonder how far you should go with these and other innovative bodies of thought. I suggest that the possible extent of embracing new knowledge is nearly limitless. You should stop only if it entails denying the truth of the Holy Bible. And you should stop only when there is a clear and undeniable conflict between new thought and the Bible, not when some pretextual conflict has been conjured up or fabricated to protect you from departing from established ways of thinking, or from the burden of thoughtful and rational analysis, or from yielding uncritically to the pressure of your peers (political correctness in current parlance).

* The co-existence of human subspecies or varieties with different cultural and intellectual attainments, as suggested in the text, is not without archaeological precedent. The Cro-Magnons and Neanderthals existed simultaneously during the final stages of the last ice age, but based on discoveries of cave art in France and flute artifacts in Germany, it is now known that only the former, and not the latter, possessed artistic and musical skills.

** Sainte Chapelle, originally a reliquary, one of the most beautiful Gothic structures of the world, was completed in 1248 A.D. by Louis IX (later Saint Louis), leader of the Seventh Crusade (1245–1250). In 1239–1241, Louis purchased twenty-two relics of the Crucifixion, including the crown of thorns, the sponge, the nails, large parts of the cross, and perhaps the spear from Emperor Baldwin II of Constantinople. These relics had been the property of the Byzantine emperors for centuries. The relics were placed inside the Grande Châsse at the altar of Sainte Chapelle. The purchase price of the relics exceeded the cost of building Sainte Chapelle. The relics were venerated and seen by thousands, with descriptions often being committed to writing for 550 years. They all were destroyed in 1791 during the French Revolution, except for the Crown of Thorns which is in the Treasury of Notre Dame Cathedral.

Chapter Three
The *P*HARISEES

*N*O LESS THAN FIFTEEN TIMES in the synoptic Gospels do we find Christ at odds with the Pharisees. The Pharisees criticized Jesus for healing on the Sabbath, for consorting with sinners, and for not fasting. Jesus exhorts His followers to avoid the hypocrisy of the Pharisees *(Luke 12:1, Matthew 16:6, Mark 8:15)*. Time after time Jesus admonishes His followers not to fall into the pharisaic narrow, blindered, close-minded, self-righteous certainty. Perhaps Christ's views of the Pharisees are best summed up in the Parable of the Pharisee in *Luke 18:10-14,* where the Pharisee self-righteously thanks God he is not an extortioner or an adulterer like other men, and reminds God that he fasts and tithes. Jesus promises that the Pharisee, like "everyone who exalts himself will be humbled." Jesus tells the Pharisees in *Mark 7:9* that they reject the commandments of God in order to honor tradition. The message of Jesus was bold and radical. The two central tenets of the Christian faith, He said, are to love God with all your heart, soul, and mind, and to love your neighbor as yourself *(Matthew 22:37)*. Yet these bedrock principles had been clearly stated in the ancient Torah *(Leviticus 19:3-4 and Deuteronomy 6:4-5)*. The Pharisees, the most doctrinaire and self-righteous of the Jewish faithful, had lost sight of their core values, and instead had concentrated on pious formalistic doctrines of Judaism.

Because Christ's revolutionary message clashed so plainly with the beliefs and practices of the Pharisees, it is not surprising that they took the lead in the persecution and crucifixion of Christ.

THE PHARISAIC CHURCH

*S*ADLY, OVER THE CENTURIES the Christian church became, if anything, more pharisaic than the Pharisees. The church was consumed with self-righteousness. The church at first suspected, then rejected and condemned, every innovative philosophy and system of thought, and the church's intolerance at its apogee spawned the Inquisition. Every person who was believed to

19

have departed from established church doctrine was tortured until he confessed his errors and then was burned to death at the stake.

Much of the impetus for the Protestant Reformation was to eradicate the Inquisition and allow people to exercise freedom of conscience and freedom of worship. Nevertheless, the Protestant denominations all too soon fell into pharisaic error, just as the old universal church had done.

Particularly, the churches refused to try to understand innovations in both physical sciences and social sciences, and instead condemned new ways of thinking. This is especially true with respect to the Copernican-Galilean discoveries of the planetary and solar bodies, the Darwinian doctrine of evolution, the principles of political freedom developed in the American Revolutionary and formative period, Freudian psychology, and the Marxist-Leninist doctrine of wealth redistribution.

By turning its back on such innovative thinking, the church drove away many of its followers, built up hostilities and even violent responses from the adherents of the new beliefs, and denied itself enrichment and nourishment that it could have received from the new thought systems.

COPERNICAN-GALILEAN ASTRONOMY

THE CHURCH FEARED THAT THE OVERTHROW of Ptolemaic astronomy by the discoveries of Copernicus and Galileo would negate the existence of heaven. A physical heaven in our plane of reference somewhere above the clouds never should have been accepted as reasonable. Once such a physical phenomenon was ruled out by astronomical discoveries, ironically there was a much better intellectual basis for belief in heaven. It now became understood that heaven must exist in a state that is not of our physical universe, but that has channels back and forth from our world for the passage of the souls of the dead, the coming and going of heavenly angels, the emanation of miracles, and the making and answering of prayers.

Galileo Galilei was a faithful Catholic his entire life. His body is buried in the nave of the Santa Croce Church in Florence. At the Vatican's insistence, he retracted his astronomical discoveries, and fortunately was neither tortured nor burned at the stake. Pope Benedict finally officially removed the Catholic Church's condemnation of Galileo at Christmas in the year 2009.

POLITICAL FREEDOM

ALTHOUGH HUMAN POLITICAL FREEDOM gained attention by theologians at least as early as the Renaissance, fully developed concepts of these ideas were a product of the eighteenth century Enlightenment. They were tentatively advanced in the Cromwellian army and political apparatus. The essential political freedoms were gradually elaborated by Hobbes, Harrington, Milton, Rousseau, Locke, Montesquieu, Jefferson, and Madison over the course of the seventeenth and eighteenth centuries. They became essentially fully formed in the American Declaration of Independence, Constitution, and Bill of Rights. I state in Chapter 7 that the Holy Spirit must have infused the Council of Nicea in 325 AD. So, too, the Holy Spirit, sent to help us and guide us to the truth as Saint John the Evangelist tells us *(John 14:16-17, 16:7-13),* must have inspired and guided the American founders in the Continental Congress, Constitutional Convention, and First Congress that produced America's fundamental political charters.

The history of development of political freedom was the history of its repression by kings, by the aristocracy, and sadly, by the church. The theologically conservative churches, Catholic and Anglican, were by far the most repressive. For example, in the Spanish dominions, the church and state formed an unholy alliance which crushed even the most modest efforts to reform either religion or politics.

It is by no means accidental that the more theologically liberal denominations, Calvinists, Baptists, Methodists, and Quakers, were the most welcoming to political reform. Indeed, it is quite logical to view the two so-called Great Awakenings of late eighteenth century and early nineteenth century American religious history, as having been inspired by the new-found political liberties of the nation. The Awakenings greatly increased church participation, but did so with an evangelistic approach that emphasized religious innovation and individualism and at the same time diminished the authority and traditions of the church. Even in the twenty-first century, we see these changes spun out, especially in the form of the non-denominational mega-church with its scantily-trained clergy, its dismissal of church history, and its reduction of doctrine and theology into mindless pop culture. The present widespread acceptance of moral relativism and situation ethics may well be attributable in large part to the over-emphasis on religious individualistic preference and de-emphasis of religious discipline and tradition inherited from the Awakenings.

Had the ancient church, the church that emphasized confession, creed, and communion, not fought to the bitter end against political freedom, no doubt it would have suffered far less of an erosion of its standing and acceptance than has been the case.

EVOLUTION

CHARLES DARWIN elaborated his theory of evolution in the mid-nineteenth century. The church fought Darwinism relentlessly. The church foolishly regarded the doctrine of evolution as being contrary to the order of divine creation. After a long struggle the evolutionists finally won, and no publicly funded school system is allowed to permit reference to any influence of God in the development of both organic and inorganic matter.

Instead, the church should have welcomed evolutionary doctrine with complete enthusiasm. There is no inconsistency whatever between scientific evolution and creation by God in the great epochs that are represented by the days of creation in the first chapter of Genesis. Appreciating the amazingly complex process of evolution only leads a person of faith to hold the God of creation in greater awe and veneration.

Evolutionary scientists at present are forced to concede that the development of life cannot be explained on the basis of totally random, unguided evolutionary

Johannes Gutenberg, *Biblia Latina,*
First page of Genesis, 1460
Gold leaf and tempura on paper.

change. Some scientists who are atheists have hypothesized that life on this planet evolved from some primitive organism transplanted here by beings from another planet. The question they cannot answer is how the alien beings themselves were created. Nor can the astrophysicists come up with an explanation of what caused the Big Bang from which the origination of the solar system is traced. They concede that this is a point which must be referred to theologians.

Also there are large gaps in several evolutionary pathways that evolutionary scientists have not been able to plug. If evidence of natural evolution to fill these gaps remains lacking, the only plausible explanation is that of God's direct intervention. Moreover, evolutionary biologists cannot begin to explain how the complexity of the human brain, especially that part of it which internalizes morality and ethics, could possibly have evolved by random natural selection, and without the tender guidance of the hand of God.

Had the church welcomed evolutionary doctrine as it should have, both religion and science would have benefitted. Intelligent, thoughtful Christians would not have been driven to atheism, and the church would not have been held up to ridicule and contempt. Also, most likely the scientific community would have been far more willing than it has been to acknowledge the divine role in creation and development of the natural order.

Because of the opposition and intransigency on both sides outlined above, there has been an unfortunate tendency on the part of Christians to regard God as somehow being bound by the laws of nature, that He surely is constrained not to depart from nature's laws. This, of course, would preclude the occurrence of miracles, and sadly, of the greatest miracle of all, the Resurrection of Jesus Christ. How can this be? We are talking about the Creator of the universe here. Surely if He has the power to have created everything and to have established the natural order, He has the power to perform miracles, by departing from that natural order whenever it is His divine will. He had the power to form the mountains, the rivers, the oceans, and all the animals and plants of the earth. Surely had the power to part the Red Sea *(Exodus 14:21-29)*, to guide Moses to bring water forth from the rock *(Exodus 17:2-6)* and to make the planet pause or slow down in its rotation during the battle of Gibeon *(Joshua 10:12-14)*.

It is no more logical to rule out miracles altogether than it is to insist that miracles ended with Christ's apparent departure from the earth. The Catholic Church has kept enormously detailed records and attestations of tens of thousands of eyewitnesses of miracles that have occurred down to contemporary times. Miracles are associated with each of the myriad saints recognized by the Catholic Church. In addition to the miracles recognized by the church, there are vast numbers of miracles that have occurred, but either did not come to the attention of the church or were not verified by its rather cumbersome processes.

If you have ever witnessed a miracle, and many of you have, you know I am speaking the truth. Even if you have had no personal experience with a miracle, it is unreasonable to deny the possibility of miracles, for this would require you to believe that all of the miracles recorded in the annals of the church, were either fabrications or hallucinations. If you accept some miracles, but deny others, where do you draw the line? And what gives you, as opposed to the collective minds and accumulated wisdom of generation after generation of church scholars, the confidence that your selections, and not the church's, are the right ones? If you accept the Resurrection, but deny the virgin birth, a not uncommon modern day position, how can you say with conviction, when you witnessed neither, that the one is true and the other is false?

The purpose of an intercessory prayer is to secure God's intervention in departing from a progression under the natural order. When God grants a prayer request, it should be regarded that a miracle has taken place. Even when prayers do not result in miraculous divine intervention, they bless both the petitioner and the person who is the object of the prayer. Prayers often include petitions for God's mercy on us, miserable sinners that we are. Thus it is fitting to invoke Shakespeare's memorable lines spoken by Portia in Act IV, Scene 1, of the *Merchant of Venice:*

> The quality of mercy is not strain'd,
> It droppeth as the gentle rain from heaven
> Upon the place beneath: it is twice bless'd,
> It blesseth him that gives, and him that takes!

When you ask for God's help in relieving someone else's affliction, the expression of concern and the generosity of what you did has a beneficial effect on your own psyche, whether or not God grants what you ask. When the object of your prayers and those of others comes to know of the prayers ascending to heaven like incense from the evening sacrifice *(Psalm 141:2)*, he is warmed and cheered, and this effect alone, according to every physician who has spoken or written on the subject, plays a material positive role in the healing process.

There is widespread belief that intercessory prayers are often, but not always, answered. This proposition had to be accepted on faith until the announcement of an interesting recent study conducted at Duke University Medical Center which appeared in the July 16, 2005, issue of *The Lancet*. The study was designed to assess the effects of prayer on patients' cures from acute heart disease.

Albrecht Dürer.
Praying Hands, 1508.
Brush in gray and black on blue prepared paper.
Vienna, Albertina.

Prayers were already being made by relatives, friends, and church congregations for a great majority of patients, so the study was essentially limited to the effects of *additional* prayers. On account of ethical rules, the patients had to be told that some of them would have additional remote prayers made for their recovery and that others would not. Thus, there was an unavoidable placebo effect in the study. Notwithstanding these confusing features of the study, the results were quite startling. The patients for whom additional prayers were made, while not experiencing better immediate outcomes from the hospital procedures, did have much lower death rates and relapse as time went on when compared to patients for whom additional prayers were not made. Of course, the placebo effect in itself is beneficial and represents some of human society's gain simply from addressing prayers to the Almighty.

Another unfortunate by-product of the rejection of God's power to create, to direct, to intervene in the development of the natural order, and to depart from the laws of nature whenever it is His desire to do so, is the tendency to worship nature, God's mere creation, rather than the Creator Himself. This is by no means a new phenomenon. Both the Old and New Testaments condemn nature worship. *Psalm 106:19-20* recounts how the children of Israel "made a calf in Horeb and worshiped a metal image. They exchanged the glory of God for the image of an ox that eats grass." Saint Paul's epistle to the *Romans, 1:22-23,* refers to how men "Claiming to be wise, … became fools and exchanged the glory of the immortal God for images resembling mortal man and birds and animals and creeping things." The early church struggled against nature worship. No less a church figure than Saint Augustine himself fell into the Manichean heresy in early adulthood, a rival faith that included a large component of nature worship.

FREUDIAN PSYCHOLOGY

Sigmund Freud offered dramatically new psychological theories near the turn of the twentieth century. Central to his psychological system were three aspects of the human mind that he labeled id, ego, and superego. The id was the seat of primitive urges and drives, essentially boiled down to the instincts of sexuality and anger. It was the ego's function to suppress these potentially destructive primordial forces and to redirect them into activities that allowed for the individual's successful functioning in human society. The work ethic and postponement of gratification, for example, are thought to be attributable to the ego. The superego was the seat of ethical and moral rules passed down from generation to generation that guided the functioning of the ego.

The church immediately reacted with hostility against Freudian psychology, and the Freudians in response tended to become atheists. Exactly the reverse is what should have happened. The church should have been grateful for these new and highly informative insights into human behavior. The church should have identified particularly with the functioning of the superego, since plainly the church is society's principal repository of ethical and moral codes. The church should have been especially grateful for the elaboration of the way by which the moral teachings of Jesus are practically applied to the events of life. Likewise, the church should have welcomed the Freudian theories on how the ego reins in and re-channels the primordial drives of violence and sexuality, both the sources of much conduct the church defines as sinful. A proper application of Freudian psychology could have been immensely supportive of the church's traditional role. Unfortunately, most of the potentially beneficial synergy was lost when the church broadly condemned Freud's work as godless and heretical.

COMMUNISM

$\mathcal{W}$HEN MARX, LENIN, AND OTHERS formulated the communist philosophy in the latter nineteenth and earlier twentieth centuries, Christianity should have immediately recognized and appreciated the consistency of communistic redistributive justice with Jesus' commands and examples that those who have wealth are absolutely obligated to share what they have with the poor. "[G]o sell what you possess and give it to the poor, and you will have treasure in heaven" *(Matthew 19:21, Mark 10:21, and Luke 18:22).*

Instead, the church became an implacable enemy of communism and the communists became resolute enemies of the church. Wherever communism came to power, with the singular exception of Poland, the church, be it Catholic or Protestant, was successfully suppressed. The churches everywhere resisted communist revolutionaries and stood at the forefront of counter-revolution, insuring even greater suppression of the faith. If Christians had welcomed communist beliefs about the need to redistribute wealth fairly, and to share equitably the limited production of the economy, would the harsh and brutal political repression that usually characterized communism, have reigned without abatement, or would there have been some amelioration of the harshness of communism? We will never know because the church did not allow for any accommodation with this new ideology. This mutual hostility ensured communism's insistence on atheism and the church's near universal rejection, not only of communism, but of democratic socialism as well.

CONCLUSION

$\mathcal{T}$HE CHURCH, THEREFORE, by being pharisaic, right in the face of Christ's many pronouncements against this vice, both weakened itself and impoverished society by its hostility against astronomical discoveries, political democracy, evolution, Freudian psychology, and communism.

Chapter Four

The TEMPLE

GOD IS IMMUTABLE, UNCHANGING, EVERLASTING. Human society constantly changes. Social change is undeniable, whether put in terms of a sort of Darwinian social evolution, or simply the effects of ever increasing learning and information garnered, passed along to succeeding generations, and by them studied, analyzed, and interpreted. Although God does not change, human perceptions of God do change as a consequence of changes in human understanding over time. Surely it cannot be argued that modern Christians are not in a position to have a fuller revelation of God than the early Israelite tribes. Modern Christians, unlike those ancient forbears, have the benefit of the New Testament, the scholarship of doctors of the church like Saint Augustine and Saint Thomas Aquinas, the writings of Martin Luther, and even more recent analyses such as those of C. S. Lewis and Deitrich Bonhoeffer.

Human conceptions and understandings of God develop over time. It is my confident belief that as time has gone on, and particularly from Christ's transfiguration and Resurrection, and as a consequence of events surrounding the Reformation, much more about God has been revealed in these later days than was perceived by the earliest followers of Yahweh. But we must not become too confident about our present understanding of God; we have but to read the Book of Revelation to realize that much mystery remains.

When our forbearers became followers of the Lord God, Our Heavenly Father, they were a nomadic people with no fixed place of abode. There could have been no concept of a permanent place of religious worship.

The earliest accounts of a formalized center of worship identified the Ark of the Covenant, originally housed within the tabernacle, a temporary structure, before the Israelites began their great journey into the Promised Land *(Exodus 25:10-25)*. On this journey the Ark of the Covenant became a portable shrine. The Ark contained the Ten Commandments and remnants of manna, the food provided by God to His people in the wilderness. It is still shocking to read the familiar Biblical passage that the shrine was so sacrosanct that when a person touched it, even accidentally, he was condemned to instantaneous death *(2 Samuel 6:6-7)*.

Just as the Ark of the Covenant was untouchable, so was God Himself unapproachable and unrevealed. He is most often represented in these times as a pillar of cloud by day and a pillar of flame by night *(Numbers 9:15-23, 14:14)*.

Not long after the people of Israel gave up their nomadic lives and settled in the Promised Land, King Solomon caused the first temple to be built at Jerusalem in the Tenth Century BC. The temple was destroyed by Nebuchadnezzar II in 586 BC.

A new temple, begun by King Herod on the same site in 19 BC, was placed in use in an unfinished state the next year, and was finally completed around 60 AD Jesus knew this temple well. He was presented at the temple on the fortieth day after His birth by Saint Joseph and the Blessed Virgin. *(Luke 2:21-35)*. He confounded the temple officials with His amazing learning and understanding when He was only 12 years old *(Luke 2:41-52)*. Early in His ministry, Jesus cleansed the temple by driving out the money changers and sellers of sacrificial animals, a rare instance of Jesus, the meek and humble One, being wrathful *(Matthew 21:12-13, Luke 19:45-48, John 2:13-25)*. Perhaps the strong feelings expressed by Jesus on this occasion had to do with His knowledge that the old system of animal sacrifices soon would be displaced by His own great eternal sacrifice of His life for the remission of the sins of us all, our ancestors, and our descendants to the end of time. Jesus taught repeatedly at the temple *(John 18:20)*. The temple's scrolls of the laws given by God to Moses were kept in the Ark inside the Holy of Holies, behind the temple curtain, accessible only by the high priest and by him only once a year *(2 Chronicles 5:7)*.

All three synoptic Gospels recount that as Jesus died upon the cross, the atmosphere became darkened, and the curtain of the temple was rent from top to bottom, thus exposing to everyone's view the theretofore forbidden Holy of Holies *(Matthew 27:51, Mark 15:38, Luke 23:45)*. Flavius Josephus *(Antiquities, Volume V, Book IV)* informs us that the heavens, the stars, and other celestial bodies were woven upon the temple curtain. Not simply a fabric curtain, but symbolically the heavens themselves, were broken open to reveal new insights of God. By this event we have an enormously powerful metaphor of the revelation of God's divine being in the person of our Savior Jesus Christ. God the Father came to be more fully revealed to us through the teachings, parables, miracles, and life and death of Christ the Son. The mysterious, inaccessible God of the Old Testament now is made manifest through Jesus Christ, whose words and deeds are preserved forever in the Gospels, who time after time physically touched, and was physically touched by, his Disciples and followers.

Jesus forecast this great change by the Transfiguration, which is recorded in all three synoptic Gospels *(Matthew 17:1-13, Mark 9:2-13, Luke 9:28-36)*. In the Transfiguration, Jesus' body and garments are illuminated and shining and God the Father speaks (one of only two times in the New Testament, the other being at Christ's baptism). The immensely and undeniably powerful message is that the shrine of Christ's body and spirit now supplant the temple as the shrine for the true worship of God.

The temple was destroyed for the last time in 70 AD as Jesus Himself had foretold *(Matthew 24:1-2)*, when a Jewish revolt was suppressed by Roman armies.

The followers of Muhammad constructed a mosque in the place of the temple. Christians in the Crusader Kingdom of Jerusalem for a time transformed the mosque into a Christian church, but their plans to tear down the mosque and replace it with a Christian basilica never came to fruition. The mosque remains today. Christians and Jews understand that to destroy the mosque now and build a temple or a church in its place would most likely be the inaugural event of World War III.

In the Holy City of Rome, it can be suggested that the leaders of the Catholic Church tried with the resplendent Saint Peters to create a substitute for the temple of Jerusalem. Yet in attempting to do that, they engaged in such grasping, greedy, and extortionate practices that Martin Luther rebelled. The Protestant Reformation resulted.

Some Christians believe that the temple will be reconstructed physically at its ancient site in Jerusalem in times associated with the Second Coming of Christ, but scriptural support for that view is weak, and it does not command a widespread acceptance among theologians. The principal texts cited to support physical reconstruction of the temple, *Ezekiel 37:26-28* and *Zechariah 6:12-15*, are fully as consistent with the views of abandonment of the need for the temple to be a physical structure that I am suggesting here. As Saint Stephen plainly said just before he was stoned to death, "[T]he Most High does not dwell in houses made by hands, …" *(Acts 7:48)*.

Jesus pointedly told us that if the temple were destroyed, He would raise it up in three days *(John 2:19)*. This prediction confounded His listeners. But now it is universally understood that He was referring to His own impending death and resurrection, not an inanimate temple constructed of stone, wood, and other physical elements.

Jesus promised those of us who believe in Him the salvation of our souls and eternal life in heaven *(John 3:16, 11:24-26)*. We understand that as we die our souls will depart our bodies instantaneously, and if our sins have been forgiven, our souls will be transported immediately to heaven.

The forty-day period between the post-Resurrection appearance of Jesus and His final Ascension is marked by His once again being with His Disciples in a physical-like form. There is a mystery surrounding His form, however. His appearance seemingly is altered so that His followers at first do not recognize Him *(Luke 24:18-20, John 20:14-16, John 21:4)*. He enters a barricaded room without making an opening *(John 20:19)*. He vanishes from the supper at Emmaus *(Luke 24:31)*. Saint Mary Magdalene is directed not to touch Him physically *(John 20:17)*, while the Apostle Thomas and others are invited to do so *(John 20:27, Luke 24:39)*. He appears in many ways to have resumed His human characteristics. He eats *(Luke 24:42)*, performs miracles *(John 21:5-6)*, and teaches the Disciples *(Luke 24:38-49, John 21:15-19, and Mark 16:15-18)*. Then He departs by being lifted up into a cloud or into the atmosphere *(Luke 24:51, Acts 1:9)*.

Nobody can provide a description of heaven, except that we have reason to believe that it is a place of light and calm. Virtually every report from someone who has come back from a near-death experience is that he was drawn into an amazingly *light* place and was overwhelmed with sensations of *calm* and *comfort*. In the words of Saint John the Evangelist (1:5), "The *light* shines in the darkness, and the darkness has not overcome it," and in the words of the Agnus Dei, the part of the ancient mass that immediately precedes the Eucharist, "Lamb of God, Who takes away the sins of the world; grant us *peace*, grant us *peace*." By contrast, other cultures describe the afterlife as a dark, shadowy, and dreary place, pervaded by an unsettled mood, anxiety or restlessness, like Hades as understood by the Greeks or Sheol as described in the Old Testament.

Heaven is some sort of sphere or plane that is in an aspect of the universe, (or is exterior to the universe) somehow tangential to the universe that we know about in a configuration that we are unable to comprehend. The resurrected and not yet ascended Christ must have been in some way within or partially within the realm of heaven. A similar heaven-earth connectivity must be the basis for events and effects not consistent with ordinary earthly functions, including the coming and going of angels, the ascension of souls from earth, the making and answering of prayers, and the occurrence of miracles.

The Disciples and Apostles expected Christ to return soon, within their own lifetimes, based on texts such as *Matthew 24:29-31, Mark 9:1* and *13:3-27,* and *Luke 21:27-28.* Yet the literal physical return of Christ seemingly did not occur then or ever. Does this make scripture wrong? No. We are told in the *Gospels of Matthew (24:36)* and *Mark (13:32)* that only God the Father, not even Jesus, knows when He will come again. To me this is an invitation either to accept being in a state of puzzlement about this, or to figure it out for ourselves in our own personal theologies.

Of course, Christ literally did come back to earth in some form or manifestation after His spirit went to heaven and His body arose from the grave. After forty days, the physical aspect of Christ ascended into heaven. Yet surely some part of Christ's spirit remained behind on earth.

One of the best focuses on Christ's remaining presence on this earth is derived from the well-known debate between Luther and Zwingli that was the unsuccessful culmination of their efforts to merge Lutheranism and Calvinism into a single Protestant church. They had been able to agree on all issues except for the Eucharist. Zwingli thought every part of Christ was in heaven and nothing of Him remained on this earth, so that it would be impossible for Him to be present in consecrated elements of communion. Luther disagreed. In exasperation, he swept away the cloth covering the table where they were seated to reveal the words of the Gospel *Matthew 26:26-28* he had written in chalk on the wood of the table: "Take, eat, this is my body…. Drink of it all of you for this is my blood…." To this day the Catholic, Eastern Orthodox, and Lutheran churches believe Christ is truly present in the consecrated elements of the Eucharist. If these more theologically traditional churches are or can be right, Jesus Christ is with us now in the midst of our earthly lives, and had been with our ancestors for more than two thousand years. There are other Protestant denominations, such as the Baptists, that de-emphasize the Eucharist, but firmly believe in Christ's presence among us in our earthly lives. In the words of the grand old Baptist hymn, "He lives, He lives,… You ask me how I know He lives? He lives within my heart."

The physical temple at Jerusalem has not been present with the Jews for two thousand years. The portable temple, the Ark of the Covenant, had not existed for at least a thousand years before that. Where is the temple now?

Recall the splendid, majestic verses of *Matthew 7:7* and *Luke 11:9,* "Ask, and it will be given to you; seek, and you will find; knock, and it will be opened to you." The widely understood meaning of these verses is that Jesus is willing to enter into all hearts, minds, and souls whenever we ask Him to do so. There is an implied corollary to these verses that Jesus is always asking to be allowed to enter into us, always seeking those of us who might yet remain the lost sheep ("And I have other sheep who are not of this fold. I must bring them also." *John 10:16*), always knocking on the doors of our hearts. When we are willing to listen to Him and when we have the will for Him to enter into our lives, He always does so. Even the thief who was crucified with Jesus and had led an evil life until the time appointed for his death, but yet who repented of his sins and believed on Jesus, was promised a passage to heaven by our Savior.

Surely the temple no longer is or will be an inanimate physical structure. Rather, the temple is within and consists of the body, mind, and soul of each believing Christian. Jesus has entered into each of these individual and personal temples, there to remain until the Christian's soul at death ascends to heaven. "Do you not know that you are God's temple…?" *(1 Corinthians 3:16).*

I argue, therefore, that the Second Coming is not some future event that nobody can predict, but that in the sense of individual temples within each faithful Christian, the Second Coming occurred right after the Resurrection, and that Jesus has remained with His faithful followers ever since, having come back immediately following the Ascension in fulfillment of the promise made by the angels in *Acts 1:11* at an unwitnessed time and place. This view is consistent with Christ's admonition in *Matthew 24:42-44* to be ready always for He is "coming at an hour you do not expect." *Mark 13:32-35* and *Luke 12:40* make the same point.

This view of the Second Coming helpfully resolves what otherwise would be a great dilemma. Christians with near uniformity believe that upon death, his soul ascends to heaven or descends to hell, so that his day of judgment is the day of his death. This is wholly inconsistent with a future Second Coming when the graves open up and both the living and dead are judged and sent to heaven or hell.* One troubling tendency on the part of some believers in an imminent Second Coming is to favor the despoliation and degradation of the environment on the theory that all will be over soon and there is no reason for conservation. Following my suggestion, in contrast, there is every reason to be good stewards of God's creation.

The Second Coming may be viewed as a timeless and endless process, not an instantaneous event. We weak and sinful humans, to do God's will, cannot act with the miraculous speed of Jesus in the performance of His miracles. He fed the five thousand by miraculously transforming a small quantity of bread and fish into a vast supply *(Mark 6:38-44, John 6:1-14)*.

Those of us who are blessed with the opportunity to farm, garden, and fish are allowed to perform similar splendid transformations, although in accordance with normal seasonal progression, not instantaneously and miraculously. We can feed thousands by raising fields of wheat and corn from a paltry quantity of seed and by catching prodigious numbers of fish originating from the spawn left by but a few of the species. These amazing natural wonders in which we are allowed to participate promise to continue so long as we are good stewards of the productive resources God has placed in our hands. Less we become too proud of our own achievements in food production we must be mindful of Saint Paul's reminder that "[N]either he who plants nor he who waters is anything, but only God who gives the growth" *(1 Corinthians 3:7)*.

Jesus instantaneously healed — restored the sick, the lame, the blind, the deaf. Over the centuries those of us who are blessed with the opportunity to provide health care service, continually and progressively have vastly improved upon the extent and speed of healing that can be accomplished. The oft-quoted label "miracle of modern medicine," of course, is an overstatement, for no matter how skillful they are, merely human health care providers cannot rival the healing transformations accomplished by Jesus. Yet, over the passage of centuries, it cannot be denied that we humans have done an increasingly better job of feeding and healing than was accomplished by our ancestors. Surely it must be that the ever-present spirit of Jesus has shaped and molded the advances in these vital human endeavors. Visit Johns Hopkins Medical Center in Baltimore sometime and stand in awe before the multistory statue of Jesus that is enclosed within the edifice of the old hospital.

The Almighty has so favored and blessed human endeavors of feeding and healing over time that the human condition has been gradually, but greatly, improved. As Adam was driven from Eden, God told him, "By the sweat of your face you shall eat bread, …" *(Genesis 3:19)*. Over countless generations most people have learned to value and honor the hard work which is necessary to earn a living and to prefer that to indolence. In this sense God's punishment has become God's reward. It may even be suggested that society's success in the developed part of the world, at least in providing for human needs, can be regarded as a process by slow stages of returning to the Garden of Eden.

When we are face to face with the poor, the sick, the naked, the homeless, the hungry, the imprisoned, we are face to face with Jesus. He has returned to this earth. He is ever with us. As Jesus Himself told us in *Matthew 25:35-40,* "For I was hungry and you gave me food, I was thirsty and you gave me drink, I was a stranger and you welcomed me, I was naked and you clothed me, I was sick and you visited me, I was in prison and you came to see me…. Truly, I say to you, as you did it to one of the least of these my brothers, you did it to me."

There is commonly thought to be a scriptural prediction that in connection with the Second Coming the graves will open up and the dead bodily shall be raised up to heaven. By no means are theologians of one mind about this. The principal textual bases, *Ezekiel 37:12-13* and *Matthew 27:52-53,* for the so-called rapture, can easily be read as relating to events surrounding not the Second Coming, but the Crucifixion, when graves did open up and saints were bodily raised from the dead. I submit that there is quite natural and longer term fulfillment of belief in the rapture in the following way. The dead are buried, their bodies decay, or if cremated, their ashes are physically and chemically transformed. They become food for micro-organisms, and then move up the animal and plant food chains until inevitably they become part of the human food supply. Human bodies are nourished, human souls are supported and sustained by their human bodies. Upon death, the souls, if saved, ascend to heaven. In this way, but only over the long course of time, graves indeed do open up and the souls nourished by the bodies do indeed ascend to heaven.

*The Last Judgment in which Christ returns to judge the living and the dead, forecast by the creeds of the Christian Church, is not founded on Scriptures, but rather on evolving church tradition. This conception, of course, is inconsistent with the now widely accepted view that souls upon death pass directly to heaven or hell. This view is also inconsistent with Christ's promise to the repentant thief on the cross, whose life had been evil up to that moment, that they would meet in paradise that very day. *Luke 23:43*. The traditional Last Judgment doctrine eventually led to the development of the purgatory dogma, thought to have been incubated by the near worldwide universal practice of praying for the dead, envisioned at first as a state of being and later becoming associated with a discrete locus, like heaven and hell. The dogma became formalized by the Councils of Lyon (1274), Florence (1438–1445) and Trent (1545–1563). A popularized version of the purgatory dogma is set forth by Dante in his *Divine Comedy* (with its parts Inferno, Purgatorio, and Paradisio). The purgatory dogma soon became the basis for the Catholic Church's practice of encouraging donations to accompany prayers for the dead. Soon, to its shame, the Church, as it sought to enlarge its power and wealth, undertook the sale of indulgences in exchange for shortening the stay of departed relatives' souls in purgatory and accelerating their admission to heaven. Of course, the sale of indulgences led directly to Luther's posting of the Ninety-five Theses and the beginning of the Protestant Reformation. Not surprisingly, Protestants, despite some equivocal pronouncements on the point by Melanchthon, Calvin, and Wesley (Philipp Melanchthon, *Apology of the Augsburg Confession*; John Calvin, *Psychopannychia*; Ted Campbell, *Methodist Doctrine: The Essentials* (1999); respectively), reject the purgatory doctrine with near uniformity. See, for example, Article XXII of the Thirty-nine Articles of Religion of the Anglican Church, which states, "The Romish Doctrine concerning Purgatory . . . is a fond thing, vainly invented, and grounded upon no warranty of Scripture, but rather repugnant to the Word of God." Also the Catholic Church has watered down considerably the purgatory dogma, John Paul II having declared in 1999 that purgatory does not indicate place but rather a condition of existence, and the Compendium of the Catechism published in 2005, defining purgatory as "the state of those who die in God's friendship, assured of their eternal salvation, but who still have need of purification to enter into the happiness of heaven."

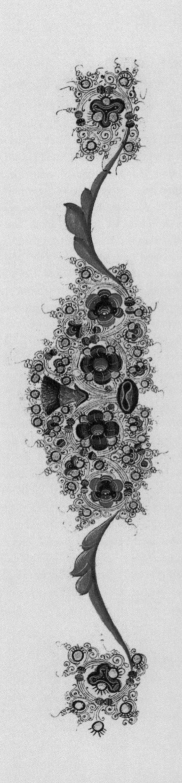

Chapter Five

SECULARITY

IN ONE OF THE MOST DEBATED AND PUZZLING of all scriptural passages, Jesus said, "Render to Caesar the things that are Caesar's and to God the things that are God's" *(Mark 12:17)*. This was in response to a question by one of the Pharisees who was trying to stake Christ out on the extent of His claimed sovereignty.

Satan had tempted Christ, offering Him not only wealth and power, but also monarchy over all the earthly kingdoms. Jesus spurned Satan's offers *(Matthew 4:1-11)*.

When Jesus was asked by Pilate whether he was king of the Jews, He declined to answer, saying only "You have said so" *(Matthew 27:11; Mark 15:2; Luke 23:3)*. Also when before Pilate Jesus stated, "My kingdom is not of this world" *(John 18:36)*.

Civil governments long predated the coming of Christ and undoubtedly will exist to the end of time. The model of civil government to which we are accustomed is one that is maintained separately from the church, as reflected in the words of the First Amendment to the United States Constitution: "Congress shall make no law respecting an establishment of religion, or prohibiting the free exercise thereof; ..." This provision is broadly understood to prohibit the state from sponsoring, aiding or supporting religious organizations, or from ceding any traditional governmental functions to religious organizations; it also prohibits governmental interference with religious organizations. Similar church-state separation provisions have been enacted by most of the governments of Western Europe.

Church-state separation is widely believed to be highly beneficial, if not imperative, to well-ordered governance in which human freedoms are respected. History has been a most powerful instructor on the relationship between church and state.

A theocracy is a state in which government is controlled by religion. Experience with theocracies over the course of time has been largely negative. Undoubtedly the least tolerable type of theocracy is one in which the government is autocratic rather than democratic. Examples of such states include modern Iran, any number of other Islamic states to a lesser degree, Central Italy while it was governed by the Papacy for several centuries, Cromwellian England, and Spain during the fifteenth and sixteenth centuries when royal authority acted in full coordination with ecclesiastical authority. The chilling episode in Act IV of Verdi's opera *Don Carlos* comes to mind, when the Grand Inquisitor reminds King Phillip II that even the king himself is subject to the Inquisition. In an autocratic theocracy, history has taught us to expect widespread denial of personal freedoms, including common use of torture and execution, and of course, rigorous suppression of any nonconforming religious belief or expression.

Democratic theocracies are unusual. The Massachusetts Bay Colony during the period of Puritan domination was a democratic theocracy. Such regimes are far less repressive than autocratic theocracies, but fall short of acceptable constitutional norms. It must not be forgotten that a number of perfectly innocent women were executed on fallacious charges of witchcraft during the period of Puritanism in Massachusetts.

The converse of theocracy is domination by an all-powerful civil government that opposes some or all religion. If that government is also autocratic, experience teaches that horrendous events can be expected. Slaughters by the millions of Christians by the French Revolutionaries and the communists of Russia, China, and Eastern Europe, as well as the murder of one-third of the world's Jewish population by the German Nazis come readily to mind.

What happens is far less clear when that civil government which opposes some or all religious activity is a democratic regime. Instances of unfairness experienced in this context include the discrimination against Catholics in England for decades following the restoration of Charles II (and even worse discrimination against Catholics in Ireland while it was administered essentially as a colony of England).

The truly perplexing problem of opposition to religion in a democratic state arises when the state attempts to displace with secular values, the values that are central to religious organizations. To some extent this appears to be occurring in contemporary America. The perceived displacement of religious values has become a great rallying focal point for the American religious right.

Yet secularization is by no means all bad. If there is one leader of the twentieth century who stood above all others, I would argue that leader was Kemal Ataturk. His government enacted modern secular laws in Turkey in the 1920's, displacing laws of the Ottoman Islamic theocracy.

The Christian and Muslim faiths in many respects have been on a collision course since the time of the founding of Islam. Christian nations all across northern Africa and central Asia, were transformed at the point of the sword into Islamic regimes. Armed struggle of epic proportions between Christian and Muslim rulers occurred for centuries in Spain and in the Holy Land. With current weapons technology, long range missiles and nuclear warheads, a renewal of Christian-Muslim armed conflict would likely result in the destruction of civilization.

J.J. Dassy.
Robert de Normandie at the Siege of Antioch 1097–1098, 1850.
CROISADES, ORIGINES ET CONSEQUENCES.

The North American and Western European nations, at one time universally Christian, have now become predominantly secular. Only between two percent and fifteen percent of the population regularly attends church. We, the western democracies, no longer have the aim, as the rulers of fifteenth and sixteenth century Spain did, of compelling the Muslims to convert back to Christianity. Instead, we would be content and would feel reasonably secure if the Islamic world became largely secular on the Turkish model. It can be argued that Indonesia, Bangladesh, Malaysia, Albania, Kosovo, Tunisia, and, ironically, pre-Gulf War Iraq are or have been largely secularized. When secularization occurs, be it in a Muslim or a Christian nation, religious fervor diminishes and the likelihood of a cataclysmic war largely disappears.

Then perhaps in one sense Jesus' admonition to allow God and Caesar to operate in their respective spheres favors secularization of societies, so that they are not propelled into warfare by their religious ardor.

Allow me to make modest prophecy at this point. The greatest secularizing event in Christian history was the Protestant Reformation. Martin Luther nailed up his *Ninety-Five Theses* in 1517, this being about 1487 years after the Crucifixion. Many people have suggested that it is time for a Muslim reformation, and that development will put a stop to the physical strife between Islam and Christianity. The great outward spread of Islam began with extensive foreign conquests around 661 AD, about thirty years after Muhammad's death. Add 1487 years and that gets you to the year 2148. But wait a minute. The Reformation really began around 1380. John Wycliffe, an English priest, declared the Pope the Anti-Christ in 1378 and in 1381 published *De Eucharistia*, which stated that the consecrated elements of the Eucharist did not become the actual flesh and blood of Christ, but rather that Christ was spiritually present in the elements. This was about 1350 years from the Crucifixion. Add 1350 to 661 and, presto, you are in the year 2011. We have all noted the popular, democratic, overwhelmingly secular uprisings in one Muslim nation after the other in 2011. Has the Islamic reformation come? Until and unless this becomes a fulfilled prophecy, it is entitled to no more credence than the prophesies of Nostradame, Jean Dixon, and a host of self-proclaimed prophets of the Protestant fringe.

The God and Caesar dichotomy has permitted Christians to abdicate much personal responsibility by rendering to God only within narrowly circumscribed aspects of their lives — those relating to the church and other directly religious aspects of life — while yielding to Caesar in all other respects. They then believe they are unfettered by the Christian moral and ethical commands in the non-religious parts of their lives. That could not be what Christ had in mind. Even the most casual study of the teachings of Jesus produces the conviction that He was prescribing a holistic code of conduct. In the simplest and most direct terms He wants us to love our neighbors as ourselves in all respects and in every phase of our behavior; and from the Parable of the Good Samaritan and His many references to our duties regarding foreigners, by neighbors He means all mankind.

To summarize the views I offer here: (1) religious organizations and organs of the state should not be allowed to control the other in any way, nor should there be any encroachment on freedom of religion; (2) secularization serves largely a beneficial interest by dulling the aggressive nature of religion; (3) Christian ethics and moral values, as distinguished from Christian practices of worship, should not be limited to our religious lives but extend to every aspect of day-to-day living. In these ways I think we best obey Christ's command to render to God what is God's and to Caesar what is Caesar's. Christianity functions not as a kingdom of this world, but rather as a heavenly kingdom, emanations from which influence our lives on earth for the good of all people by means of voluntarily performed good acts, not acts compelled by law and under pain of punishment.

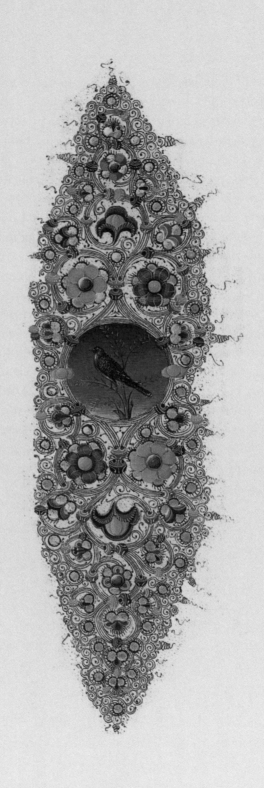

Chapter Six
DE EUCHARISTIA

BUT ONE OF THE SOLDIERS PIERCED HIS SIDE WITH A SPEAR, AND AT ONCE THERE CAME OUT BLOOD AND WATER *(John 19:34).*

SAINT JOHN THE EVANGELIST is the only one of the Gospel writers to record the flowing of blood and water from Jesus' body. He was the only one of the Gospel writers who personally witnessed the Crucifixion *(John 19:35).*

This occurrence contains the seeds and shoots of reconciliation between Catholicism and Protestantism over the sacrament of the Eucharist.

The Catholic Church always believed, and still believes, that a physical miracle occurs at each celebration of the Eucharist, that the consecrated elements become the actual body and blood of our Savior. More conservative Protestants accept John Wycliffe's pronouncement in the year 1381 in his work *De Eucharistia,* that Christ is only spiritually present in the consecrated elements. Luther was in essential agreement.

The Calvinists and the most mainline Protestant denominations today, on the other hand, look upon the consecrated elements simply as symbolic of Christ. We are reminded of the epic confrontation between Luther and Zwingli on this subject. They met with the goal of unifying Protestantism. The only issue on which they could not agree was Christ's presence or absence in the Lord's Supper. Zwingli insisted that Christ was far away in the domain of heaven. Luther insisted that Christ was truly present in the consecrated elements. Luther in exasperation pulled away the cloth covering the table between them to reveal words from the Gospel he had inscribed in chalk: "Take, eat, this is my body. . . . Drink of it all of you for this is my blood" *(Matthew 26:26-28).*

Is there any way to reconcile the Catholic belief in miraculous conversion of the consecrated elements into Christ's body and blood, with the conservative Protestant belief that Christ is spiritually present in the bread and wine? I submit that *John 19:34* leads us to the reconciliation.

Golgotha was a rugged place, but surely it supported tufts of dried grass and wild vines including grape vines. Grass when it is dry looks dead, but these looks are deceiving, for the plants continue to possess vitality long after the blades above the ground seem dead as the chlorophyll and sap in the leaves simply retreat into the root system. Splash a bit of water on a dry tuft of grass, and in three days or so, the dried leaves are suddenly green and vital again. The metaphor here of Christ's own death and after three days, Resurrection, is quite apparent.

The water that sprang from the pierced side of Jesus easily could have fallen on a patch of dry grass. Then in three days or so, about the time of Jesus' Resurrection, the dried grass would have grown green again.

It is tempting, far too tempting, to think that the revitalized grass watered from Jesus' own body was wheat from which would come the Eucharistic wafer — for wheat, indeed all grain and even maize or corn, are part of the great botanical grass family, Graminiae. More likely, however, the route to the Eucharistic element was more round-about. Rather than wheat, the grass was likely of a variety that eventually produced seed heads, but not of a kind that were part of the human diet. Since all available greenery in this semi-arid land was browsed by livestock, more likely and before maturing and seeding out, the shoots of grass would have been consumed by a ruminant: a donkey, a cow, a goat, or most likely of all, a lamb, these being by far the most numerous of the domestic herbivores.

Jan van Eyck.
The Ghent Altarpiece: The Adoration of the Lamb (1432).
Oil on wood panel.
GHENT, ST. BAVO CATHEDRAL.

Yes, a lamb. Remember that Jesus was the Lamb of God *(John 1:29, 36)*. This calls to mind perhaps the greatest of all iconic masterpieces of the Renaissance, Jan van Eyck's *Adoration of the Lamb* altarpiece at St. Bavo Cathedral in Ghent. But Jesus had a dual role, that of the Good Shepherd, as well *(John 10:11, 12, 14)*. In perhaps the last recorded event in Jesus' forty days after the Resurrection and before the Ascension, He asked Peter, the rock on which the church was to be founded *(Matthew 16:18)*, three times if he loved Jesus, and upon receiving affirmative assurances, Jesus thrice enjoined Peter, "Feed my lambs. . . . Tend my sheep. . . . Feed my sheep." Christ's references to His sheep unquestionably were to the members of the Christian church *(John 21:15-17)*.

It is extraordinarily meaningful, then that Jesus, Himself the Lamb who gave His life to relieve humankind from its burden of sin, should have produced water from His dying body that nourished grass and made it the source of food for lambs.

Part of that grass would have passed through the lamb's alimentary canal and would have been deposited as droppings on the ground. Livestock manure was not looked upon as unattractive litter, as it is now, but was prized for its nourishing qualities. Every manure deposit was carefully scooped up and spread on fields of grain or other crops. Thus, in this attenuated way, the water that flowed from Jesus' side in part would have been deposited on a grain field, a field of wheat quite probably.

The wheat eventually would have been harvested, winnowed, ground, and baked into bread. In response to the words of institution in all four Gospels, *Matthew 26:26-29, Mark 14:22-25, Luke 22:14-23*, and *John 6:48-58*, some of the bread would have become the consecrated host of a communion in the early Christian church. The best of the wheat, however, would have been carefully dried and stored, zealously protected from rodents, insects, and other destroyers, and planted in the ground for the next year's crop. And so on, from generation to generation, century to century. The precious seed grain in ancient days would not even be consumed in times of hunger or famine, for to do so, would have precluded next year's crop and the crops for years thereafter.

At the prehistoric beginning of human grain farming, the grasses yielding grain heads were perennials. But before the dawn of recorded history, grass grains were bred to become annuals, with the roots dying about the time of harvest. At present, plant breeders are working with alchemistic intensity, but hopefully with greater probability of success than alchemy, to develop good yielding perennial grains. The savings of energy from tillage and the prevention of soil and water erosion from such a development are obvious.

So it was in generation after generation, century after century, seed from seed, going back to the time of the Crucifixion in a continuous cycle providing the flour for the Eucharistic bread. Truly we can say that the water that flowed from Christ's side is genetically present in the wafer of the present day Eucharist. Catholic and Protestant differences on the subject become wholly irrelevant in this conception of the Eucharistic host.

Blood flowed from Christ's side. Blood is perhaps the best fertilizer ever known. Dried blood is an essential ingredient of modern organic fertilizers. It is not unlikely that some of Christ's blood flowed on a grapevine at the foot of the cross. Unlike grain, which breeds true from seed, grapevines almost always produce useless fruits that are small, bitter, sour, and subject to rapid decay. Only the extremely rare vine yields good grapes to eat or to press for wine. In the grapevine culture analogy in *Saint John's Gospel, 15:1-7,* we are told that Jesus is the vine and God is the vinedresser. For the vineyard to succeed, however, human intervention by means of grafting is necessary. Shoots from good grapes are grafted by human hands into rootstock in order to produce edible grapes and drinkable wines. The grafting shoots are known as scions, literally "sons."

Thus, to produce wine for the Eucharist, human involvement by means of grafting is essential, just as human hearts, hands, and voices are necessary for the survival and vitality of God's church on earth. The process of grafting scions into rootstock has gone from generation to generation, century to century. As Mediterranean culture advanced into first Southern and then Northern Europe, the vine was brought along, both rootstock and scion. That ancient vine from Golgotha, fertilized by Christ's blood, most likely is genetically present in various vineyards in the Mediterranean littoral and in grape growing regions around the world.

Just as it was with the Eucharistic bread, so it is with the Eucharistic wine, genetically Christ's blood being transmitted into modern day vines, which grow grapes from which the wine for Holy Communion is made. Here, too, the differences disappear between Catholic and Protestant beliefs about Communion.

Just as the church is dependent for its survival on generation after generation of clergy in apostolic succession going back to Christ's laying His hands on the Disciples, so it is dependent for its Communion service on generation after generation of grain and grape growers, who carefully gather and guard the seed of the season's harvest for the next year's planting, and who carefully graft the scion from the good vine into the rootstock to insure the harvest of good grain and grapes that become the Eucharistic bread and wine.

In conclusion, we may say with good reason that, regardless of whether or not the consecrated elements of each Eucharistic celebration undergo miraculous transformation, the blood and water that miraculously flowed from Christ's side have been genetically transmitted over the centuries, with each new spring's seedlings and shoots, as part of God's natural order that is so beautiful and complex as to seem miraculous, and that somewhere in Christendom, even today, a congregation partaking of Holy Communion ingests the fruits of the flow of life sustaining fluids from Christ's body.

Chapter Seven
JESUS' BEST FRIEND

HOW OFTEN WE TRADITIONAL CHRISTIANS in our conversations with one another agree that anyone who does not worship Jesus Christ cannot possibly enter the kingdom of heaven. Yet we really deep in our hearts do not believe that. Surely if we did, we would do our utmost to convert our Jewish, Unitarian, Muslim, and agnostic friends, or at least seriously warn them of the imminent threat of eternity in hell. Yet we do not. Here is why we do not.

The writings of the Apostle John are immensely important. He was "the disciple whom Jesus loved" *(John 19:26, 21:7, 20)*. In Medieval and Renaissance art he is invariably present, along with the Blessed Virgin, at the crucifixion, based on the text *John 19:26*. Jesus at the crucifixion told Saint John to regard the Virgin as his mother, and Saint John took her into his own home *(John 19:27)*. He was the only one of the twelve not to meet a violent death. He lived to an old age.

Saint John, of all the Gospel writers, makes it the clearest that Jesus is divine and that the only way to the Father is through Christ. "I am the way, and the truth, and the light. No one comes to the Father except through me" *(John 14:6)*. Indeed, Jesus and God are in and of one another. "I and the Father are one" *(John 10:30)*. "I am in the Father and the Father is in me." *(John 14:10, 17:21)*.

The Gospel of John commences with the familiar words: "In the beginning was the Word, and the Word was with God, and the Word was God" *(John 1:1)*. It is universally believed that Word means Jesus, and it is not my intention to dispute that. The Greek text of Saint John's Gospel uses the word *logos*, which can only be translated as "word." No imaginable construction or spin can make it come out any other way. Saint John's Gospel is written with precision. The necessary conclusion is that John here deliberately focuses on the message of Jesus, rather than on His personhood. At the beginning of this Gospel we are told Jesus' message: to unfold through His teachings, His parables, and His miracles and good deeds, is of essential and paramount importance to Christianity. As Jesus says in the high priestly prayer, "I have given them the words that you gave me, and they have received them ..." *(John 17:8).*

The most quoted verse of *Saint John's Gospel, 3:16,* "For God so loved the world, that he gave his only Son, that whoever believes in him should not perish but have eternal life," suggests that the belief in Christ's person is that which is essential. Yet we are told clearly in verse *5:24* "whoever hears my word and believes him who sent me has eternal life." It is, therefore, belief in the message of Christ, not merely the worship of his person, that may earn salvation. Also Jesus seeks to deflect worship of Himself back to worship of God in verse *12:44* where he says, "Whoever believes in me, believes not in me, but in him who sent me."

The only prayer that Jesus prescribed, the Lord's Prayer *(Matthew 6:9, Luke 11:2),* could be recited in good conscience by any member of a monotheistic faith that did not accept the divinity of Christ, since it is a petition addressed solely to God Almighty, making declarations and asking for help in ways that are common to most major religions, and does not even invoke Jesus' name.

Jesus gave his followers a simple summary of his theology in *Matthew 22:37,* "You shall love the Lord your God with all your heart and with all your soul and with all your mind. This is the great and first commandment. And a second is like it: you shall love your neighbor as yourself." In Saint John's Gospel the centrality of loving one another is clearly and repeatedly stated *(John 13:34, 15:12).* Although loving your neighbor is the essential element of Christianity, this mandate first appears in the ancient Mosaic law. The *Book of Leviticus* is the middle book of the Pentateuch, and near the middle of *Leviticus,* verse *19:18,* it is stated "you shall love your neighbor as yourself."

Saint John's Gospel sets forth an explanation of how the Christian faith strengthens and prospers by invoking the analogy of viniculture. "I am the vine, and my Father is the vinedresser. Every branch in me that does not bear fruit he takes away, and every branch that does bear fruit he prunes, that it may bear more fruit.... Abide in me, and I in you. As the branch cannot bear fruit by itself, unless it abides in the vine, neither can you, unless you abide in me. I am the vine; you are the branches. Whoever abides in me and I in him, he it is that bears much fruit, for apart from me you can do nothing.... If you abide in me, and my words abide in you, ask whatever you wish, and it will be done for you" *(John 15:1-7).*

In this vital passage, we are not told what the grapes are. God is the vinedresser, Jesus is the vine, the Christian believers are the fruiting branches, but what are the grapes? The Gospel leaves that for us to figure out. I suggest that the grapes are the moral and ethical values embodied in Christ's life and ministry.

Jesus told us concerning His moral and ethical rules, "My yoke is easy, and my burden is light" *(Matthew 11:30).* While endlessly varying lists of these rules could be made, the following is gleaned from a superficial reading of the Gospel of Matthew, saint and Disciple of Christ: worship God, have faith, be a witness to your faith but do not seek recognition for your good deeds, and undergo persecution if necessary. Feed the hungry, give drink to those who thirst, clothe the naked, give and lend to those in need, try to heal the sick, minister to the blind and the deaf and the lame, try to help the mentally ill to recover (drive out evil spirits), provide for the little children, be kind to strangers and be kind to prisoners. Love your enemies, be a peacemaker, forgive, do not anger or be vengeful, do not condemn or judge others, show mercy, reconcile with and satisfy your accusers. Do not murder, steal, lie, slander, envy, commit adultery, be lustful or engage in sexual immorality. Honor your father and mother. Do not accumulate wealth, or be self-indulgent or greedy, and do not be obsessive about material needs. Be meek, humble; be a servant and not a master.

Perhaps a good way to test the proposition that the grapes are the moral and ethical values embodied in Christ's life and ministry would be to examine what happens in societies that make a deliberate effort to overthrow the Christian church. What happens is the ultimate form of ill-treatment of your neighbor — mass murder and genocide, and not only the extermination of Christians. During the seven great persecutions in the pre-Constantine Roman Empire, there were massive killings. During the French Revolution, when the state tried to suppress wholly the church, millions were slaughtered. When the communists in Russia decreed an atheistic society, tens of millions were executed. When the Nazis abandoned Christianity in favor of a revival of ancient Norse deities, millions were martyred, including a third of the world's Jewish population.

Although they tried mightily to do so, the persecutors — the Roman government, the French Revolutionaries, the Muslims, the Nazis, the communists — could not succeed in obliterating Christianity. Christianity not only survived, but was also strengthened. When the faith was at its smallest and weakest stage, there were seven great persecutions, all of them unsuccessful. You know about the wild animals tearing Christians apart in the Coliseum and Roman troops trapping them in the catacombs and spearing or slashing them to death. For a contemporary account of the systematic grinding down of the Christian faithful, refer to the 97th Epistle of Pliny the Younger, written around 110 AD, while serving as governor of Bithynia to the Emperor Trajan:

> I have asked them, if they were Christians.... When they have persevered, I have put my threats into execution. For I did not in the least doubt, that whatever their confession might be, their audacious behaviour, and immovable obstinacy required absolute punishment....
>
> Others of them ... have said, that they were Christians, ... but had now entirely renounced their error.... All these worshipped your image, and the images of the gods; and they vented imprecations against Christ....
>
> I thought it more necessary to try to gain the truth even by torture, from two women, who were said to officiate at their worship. But I could discover only an obstinate kind of superstition, ...

The point is that Christian ethics and morality, the grapes, are dependent for their vitality on members of Christian churches, the fruiting branches of the body of Christ, being able to function freely in society. Without the nourishment of ethics and morality by persons committed to Jesus, these essential social values atrophy. They fail to form, or wither or rot. The consequence is widespread killings and all kinds of inhuman behavior.

In this day and time there is much opposition to organized religion. There are powerful secular forces at work in the educational system and society at large which oppose the church and seek to diminish its influence. Yet, as long as a committed, relatively small minority of Christians are active, the grapes, that is, ethical and moral values traditionally identified with Christianity, seem to remain relatively healthy.

This proposition can be tested by posing the question: Where else in the world would we as Americans feel comfortable and secure in living if we were required to leave America? The answer invariably includes Canada and New

Zealand, almost always Great Britain and Australia, and then often extends to such northern European countries as Ireland, Germany, Netherlands, Denmark, Sweden, Finland, and Norway. All of these countries are traditionally Christian. All of them have as the dominant church, a credal, communing, confessional denomination — United States (Catholic), New Zealand (Anglican), Canada (Catholic and Anglican), Great Britain (Anglican), Australia (Anglican), Ireland (Catholic), Netherlands (Catholic), Germany (Lutheran and Catholic), Denmark (Lutheran), Norway (Lutheran), Sweden (Lutheran), and Finland (Lutheran). While enrolled church attending people amount to about fifteen percent of the United States population, they range from two percent to five percent in the other countries just mentioned. We would be willing to live in these countries because we can count on the norms of Christian ethics and morality to prevail there. One lesson from this analysis is that only a small portion of the population need be included among the fruiting branches of the vine in order for the grapes to be healthy and abundant.

Another lesson in this analysis is that non-Christians in a traditionally Christian nation, be they agnostics, Jews, Unitarians, or Muslims, are ordinarily willing to abide by the prevailing social rules and norms that are nothing but the old Christian ethical and moral values. Imam Feisal Abdul Rauf led the effort in 2010 to establish a Muslim community center two blocks from the World Trade Center site. He asked Muslims to be conciliatory toward Christians and Jews, denounced terrorism, stated that killing civilians is contrary to Islam, and asserted that there is a congruence of American democracy and Islam. Another example from 2010 involved a fundamentalist Christian minister's stated intention to burn Korans. He was talked out of doing this mainly by Imam Muhammad Musri, president of the Islamic Society of Central Florida, who stressed the need for tolerance and mutual respect in religious matters, and even attempted to persuade Imam Rauf to relocate the Islamic center away from the site of the towers in deference to concerns of Christians. These Muslim leaders reflect the benign and pacifying effect of the predominant Christian morality and ethics in our society. In countries of the Muslim heartland, by contrast, conversion to Christianity results in a death sentence, disrespect of the Koran (not even burning it) is subject to grave punishment, and it is unlawful to have Christian churches, schools, and other institutions.

Why then is it so essential that Christ in His person be worshiped as a deity, a member of the Holy Trinity of God? Jesus did not command His own deification in the Gospels, as He easily could have. The closest He seems to have come to that is in the words of institution of the Holy Communion. He tells the Disciples in the synoptic Gospels, and everyone in the Gospel of John, to eat of His body and drink of His blood *(Matthew 26:26-29; Mark 14:22-25; Luke 22:14-23; John 6:48-58)*. Significantly, Saint John's Gospel omits the account of the Lord's Supper, and focuses instead, at the final gathering of His intimate followers, on Jesus washing His disciples' feet *(13:4-17)*. Jesus does not command that He Himself be worshiped. Instead, most frequently He describes Himself as the Son of Man (thirty times in Matthew, thirteen times in Mark, twenty-five times in Luke, and eleven times in John, for a total of seventy-nine times in the Gospels), and in the powerful passage from Saint John's Gospel just mentioned, He portrays Himself as the servant of the faithful, not their master.

The criticality of worshiping Jesus as a divine being springs not from the New Testament, but instead emerges from the lessons of the early history of the church. Christianity could have gone off in various directions that would have insured either its doom or its relegation to the status of a minor sect.

Just after the crucifixion, the early Christian followers were leaderless and unsure of what direction to take. The Gnostic gospel of Saint Mary Magdalene, while it cannot be accepted as authoritative, contains a fascinating account of how she organized, energized, and emboldened the fragmented Christian community. Of course, as thoroughly shown in the Epistles, we have Saint Paul to thank primarily for shepherding the fragile church through its critical formative stages.

Many early Christians thought that they should be regarded simply as a refinement or advancement of Judaism. The Book of Galatians recounts Saint Paul's struggles with that church to overcome this characterization of the Christian faith. In contrast, Gnosticism sought to blend Christianity into a sort of primitive universalism that was consistent with higher forms of Hellenistic thought. The Christian struggle against Gnosticism is reflected in the Book of Colossians.

In the early centuries of the Christian era there were well-documented major trends for the church to become unitarian, on one hand, or polytheistic, on the other. Saint Athanasius labored mightily and largely successfully against the Arian heresy, a primitive form of Unitarianism that denied the divinity of Christ. He was a principal drafter of the Nicene Creed. Arianism eventually died out by the seventh century.

The struggle in the early church over the correct understanding of the status of Jesus is reflected in a legendary dispute between Sabianus and Sylvanus, Archbishop of Nazareth, just after the death of Saint Jerome in 420 AD. Sabianus argued that Jesus had a dual nature, human and divine, relying on a purported letter from Saint Jerome. Sylvanus claimed the letter was a fake. It was agreed that if divine intervention occurred overnight proving the letter to be a forgery, Sylvanus would lose his head, and if not, Sabianus would have his head struck off. Morning arrived without a sign from God. As Sylvanus knelt before the executioner, Saint Jerome appeared in the sky, arrested the sword of the executioner, and denounced Sabianus, whose head miraculously fell from his body. All of Sabianus's followers converted to Christianity.

Raphael (Italian, 1483-1520).
St. Jerome Saving Sylvanus and Punishing Heretic Sabianus, 1502-1503.
Oil on panel.
NORTH CAROLINA MUSEUM OF ART, RALEIGH.

Purchased with funds from Mrs. Nancy Susan Reynolds, the Sarah Graham Foundation,
Julius H. Weitzner, and the State of North Carolina.

Second in succession as Roman emperor after Constantine, was Julian the Apostate, who came near to re-establishing paganism, but fortunately his successor Jovian was an orthodox Christian. Saint Paul warned the early church against return to polytheism in *1 Corinthians 3:4-6.* Pope Damasus I (336 to 384 AD) is remembered for having pandered to the Roman masses in their zeal to worship saints and martyrs as a sort of substitute for the polytheism they had known. This supposed tendency on the part of the Roman Catholic Church was one that remained troubling to many Christians even into recent times. Of course, Catholicism's veneration of, and prayer through, the saints was one of the major issues of the Reformation.

Jesus in Saint John's Gospel foretells the coming of the Holy Spirit, not as some mysterious ill-defined force, but in the capacity of a "Helper" and as the "Spirit of truth" *(14:16-17, 16:7-13).*

If ever a human assembly was permeated and infused by the Holy Spirit, it was the Council of Nicaea, 325 AD, which adopted the Nicene Creed, making formal the worship of Christ and the Holy Spirit, members of the triune God; which specified from amongst the dozens of gospels and epistles, the canonical texts of the Bible, and which fixed baptism, confession, and the Eucharist as the lynchpins of Christian worship. It is important to recognize, however, that the Council of Nicea did not write upon a clean slate. The canonical texts of the Bible had been largely agreed upon by the second century church, at least that part of it not infected with the Arian, Gnostic, and Manichean heresies. We are indebted to Pliny the Younger, writing around 110 AD, for a description of the Christian worship service: "to sing alternately among themselves hymns to Christ, as to a God; binding themselves by oath, not to be guilty of any wickedness; not to steal, nor to rob; not to commit adultery, nor break their faith when plighted; nor to deny the deposites in their hands, ..." Thus, these very early Christian ceremonies contained both components identified in this chapter: worship of Christ's person and pledge to keep Christ's moral and ethical teachings.

Therefore it was not the pronouncements of Christ in the Gospels, but rather the real life experiences of the early church that determined it to be essential for the survival of the church, the new growth from which the grapes spring forth, to worship the person of Christ. Without this form of worship, the grapes, the ethical and moral rules underpinning society, are destined to wither or rot. The good news is, as modern experience has taught us, that even a small minority of communal, credal, confessional Christians can function successfully as the new growth of the vine, whose fruiting branches produce ever anew in each generation fully formed healthy crops of grapes.

These traditional Christians do not feel they are making sacrifices to perform such functions; they do so joyfully and contentedly. They, as all of us do, lapse into sin. Some are so sinful and have strayed so far from the common body of ethical and moral rules that they are regarded to be religious but immoral. Great numbers of others, be they Jews, Muslims, Unitarians, agnostics, Buddhists, or Hindus, may adhere quite closely to the common body of moral and ethical rules that are central to Christianity. Many of these persons are moral but without traditional Christian faith. To choose between the two is not difficult; the person who is moral and ethical without being religious, he or she who cherishes the grapes as defined here, surely is superior to the person who is religious without being moral and ethical, in the eyes of both God and humankind.

Therefore, there are many pathways to a life pleasing to God. I personally prefer the pathway of Missouri Synod Lutheranism, and would be quite content if the ancient universal church had only been reformed, as Desiderius Erasmus and Philipp Melanchthon would have suggested, to substitute congregational polity for ecclesiastical hierarchy, married pastors for celibate priests, and Jesus Christ as the only mediator and advocate with the Heavenly Father, with the saints deserving of respect but not worshiped. For others there are equally satisfying and successful pathways, be it Judaism, Roman Catholicism, Eastern Orthodoxy, one of the numerous sects of Protestantism, Islam, Hinduism, or Buddhism.

Chapter Eight
The $\mathcal{M}$OTHER *and* $\mathcal{B}$ROTHER *of* $\mathcal{J}$ESUS

$\mathcal{W}$E SHOULD PAY PARTICULAR ATTENTION to the lives and records of the members of Christ's own nuclear family. From them we can gain insight into the truth of Christianity that is not necessarily derivable from the writings and recorded deeds of His Disciples.

Yet, there were other members of Jesus' nuclear family, not only His stepfather Saint Joseph, but also half brothers (in addition to James) Joses, Judas, and Simon, and half sisters whose names and number are not recorded *(Matthew 13:55)*. Dan Brown in *The Da Vinci Code,* in many respects a book that attacks and undermines the Christian faith, makes the preposterous suggestion that Jesus and Saint Mary Magdalene, whether or not married, had a child, and from that child came a single line of descendants, one of whom is alive at present. Not even the Gnostic Gospel of Mary Magdalene makes such a bizarre claim. Perhaps Jesus did have a romantic attachment to Saint Mary Magdalene, but even that notion seems to rest in part on the conflation of Saint Mary Magdalene with Saint Mary, the sister of Saint Martha, about whom there are accounts of her sitting at Jesus' feet and raptly listening to His teachings, anointing Him with ointment, and drying His feet with her hair *(Luke 10:39, John 11:2)*. Surely if Jesus had been married at least one of the Gospels would have mentioned that vital biographical fact. Therefore, we should be inclined to reject the idea that Jesus left any children behind.

With His brothers and sisters, however, matters are different. More likely than not some of them married and had children. Even Saint James the Younger could have been married and a father, since he died a martyr's death about thirty years after Jesus' Crucifixion, according to the historian Hegesippas.

Instead of the slender single line of descent from each of the half siblings that Dan Brown, to be consistent, would suggest, the gene pool of all of Europe, North America, the entire Mediterranean Basin, and much of the remainder of Asia and Africa, and Latin America as well, most likely contains genetic material passed down from Jesus' half siblings. Indeed, only certain remote and relict populations would be totally free from the genes of the family of Christ.

Intensive genetic studies within the Jewish population in the last two decades support this conclusion. Contemporary Jewish descendants from the priestly caste, most of whom bear some variant of the surname Cohen, are found mostly to be descended from the "Y-chromosomal Aaron," a common ancestor who lived at the time assigned in the Bible to Aaron, the first high priest and brother of Moses.* The Jewish Diaspora into Europe, North Africa, and Asia took place after the destruction of the Temple in 70 AD. The genes of about half of all modern Ashkenazi Jews, a population of eight million, are traceable to four women who lived in Europe one thousand years ago.** Despite the efforts of Jewish society to maintain its purity, on pain of expulsion from family and community in the event of marriage to a non-Jew, strong genetic ties to non-Jewish groups have been found, including Italians, French, Slavs, Kurds, Druze, and Bedouins.*** Unlike Jewish society, which strove to maintain its purity, Jews who converted to Christianity, presumably including the half siblings of Jesus, were enjoined to go into all the world and spread the Gospel, and were under no constraints against intermarriage with Gentiles the world over.

From this research we learn that human genetic material is very persistent in lines of descent, widespread dispersal of genetic materials occurs at astonishingly rapid rates, and Jewish genetic material passes easily into non-Jewish populations (much of this assimilation no doubt being attributable to Christianized Jews). It is reasonable to believe, therefore, that within the one hundred or so generations that have passed since Christ's life, genes derived from His half siblings have been thoroughly and widely mixed into the gene pool throughout much of the world.

This concept of human interrelatedness is beautifully supported in imagery of the Messianic prophecy in *Isaiah 11:1-2*:

There shall come forth a shoot from the
	stump of Jesse,
and a branch from his roots shall bear fruit.
And the Spirit of the Lord shall rest upon
	him,
the Spirit of wisdom and understanding,

the Spirit of counsel and might,
the Spirit of knowledge and the fear of the
Lord. . . .

Isaiah here refers to a pollarded stump, where a tree has been cut deliberately to provide a nursery, so to speak, for a crop of useful wooden materials
— timbers, poles, staffs and rods — that form a multi-pronged ring around
the stump. This silvicultural phenomenon points to the reality that not just
a single line of descent from King David, but rather multiple lines of descent
from him have come into being. Thus, all of us likely are descended from
King David, just as we are descended from Abraham.

The genealogies of Jesus Christ are set out in the First Chapter of Matthew
and the Third Chapter of Luke. They begin with Abraham and Adam, respectively, and end, not with the Virgin Mary, the biological mother of Jesus,
but rather with Saint Joseph, Jesus' stepfather. The relevance of this genealogy
has been puzzling to many students of the Bible. Truly, the New Testament
genealogies are crucially relevant to Christians today and of all times; for it is
through Saint Joseph and the Blessed Virgin and their children, half siblings of
Jesus, that many of us are likely descended.

Jesus' self-references were more often to Son of Man than any other name.
In fact, He refers to Himself as the Son of Man no less than seventy-nine times
in the Gospels. The number seventy-nine is of rich Judeo-Christian numerological significance, a trinitarian number, being the sum of the product of six (days
of Creation without the day of rest) and twelve (tribes of Israel, Disciples) plus
seven, an immensely important number as noted in the Appendix. Jesus as Son
of Man implies that He is not only our Savior, but also our Brother, and He is
our Brother, not just metaphorically, but also in fact on account of the genes
within us that came from His half brothers and half sisters. So, too, do our fellow congregants, to whom we fondly refer as our brothers and sisters in Christ,
likely bear, not merely a figurative, but a factual, relationship with us.

THE BLESSED VIRGIN, MOTHER OF JESUS

THE VIRGIN MARY KNEW the essential truths of Christ's main teachings as
soon as He was conceived in her womb. In the Magnificat, Mary declares:
he has scattered the proud in

the thoughts of their hearts;
he has brought down the mighty from
their thrones
and exalted those of humble estate;
he has filled the hungry with good things,
and the rich he has sent away empty.
(Luke 1:51-53).

At the beginning of His ministry, Jesus attends the wedding at Cana. The Virgin Mary is present. When Mary tells Him that they have run out of wine, He protests that this is not His concern, that His hour has not yet come. Only with Mary's urging does Jesus perform His first miracle of transforming water into wine *(John 2:1-9).*

When all of the Disciples, except Saint John, fled at the time of the carrying of the cross and the Crucifixion, the Blessed Virgin remained with Him every step of the way, as did Saint Mary Magdalene, and at least two other women close to Jesus. Some of the women buried Him. Saint Mary Magdalene and one or more other women were the ones who found the tomb empty on the third day, so discovering the Resurrection *(Matthew 27:55, 61, 28:1-6; Mark 15:40, 47, 16:1-4; Luke 23:28-29, 55, 24:1-3, 10; John 19:25, 20:1).*

The rise of the Virgin Mary in importance in the Catholic Church over time conceivably mirrored or was mirrored by the increasingly elevated status of women generally.

Now especially those of us who are Protestants have difficulty conceiving the elevated status of the Virgin in the late-Renaissance church. Over the centuries she had attained the highest possible standing short of being a divinity. Prayers and petitions were directed to her with as much frequency and fervency as those addressed to the Heavenly Father and to Jesus Christ. Major chapels dedicated to the veneration of the Virgin had been added to cathedrals and principal churches. Among the most important festivals of the church year were those of the Annunciation, the Assumption, and the Coronation of the Virgin. She was regarded to be the Queen of Heaven.

For Protestants, all of this ended with the Reformation. In the more traditional Protestant sects, the Virgin was reduced to a status no greater than that of the Twelve Apostles; and in the less formal denominations, she was largely disregarded.

The vastly enhanced role of the Virgin in Renaissance worship was emblematic of a broader acceptance of an advanced status of women in contemporary society.

Christianity is unique among the major religions of the world with respect to protection of women. The acceptance of women as important respected members of the Christian community is made manifest in the Gospels. Christianity departed abruptly from the practices of other contemporary societies that demeaned, degraded, and enslaved women. Jews and barbarians alike permitted the taking of multiple wives, an extreme form of the debasement of women. All contemporary societies, as was particularly demonstrated by the highest orders of Roman imperial society, allowed instantaneous and groundless divorces. Early Christians labored mightily to reverse these abominable practices. The *Gospel of Matthew (19:9)*, addressed as it was to Jewish proselytes, made it clear that remarriage was sinful, when it followed divorce for a reason other than adultery. Lifetime monogamous marriage became the golden standard of Christian society.

Throughout all times mothers have been the protectors of children. The rule of lifetime monogamous marriage, to be sure, gives maximal security to the child-rearing mother, since it insures continued support and protection of the child by the father. At the dawn of the Christian era, male predators of defenseless children of both sexes reached the most extreme level of depravity. Turn to Tacitus, Suetonius, and Petronius, if your stomach is strong enough, and read lurid accounts of how Romans from the emperor on down regularly committed sexually predatory acts on defenseless children. The followers of Jesus, remembering his words, "Let the little children come to me ... for to such belongs the kingdom of heaven" *(Matthew 19:14)*, rejected these horrible practices, and one of the hallmarks of the ancient Christian church was its protection of children.

Certainly, we would not have had a Christian religion at all had not the Blessed Virgin and Saint Joseph tenderly conducted the infant Jesus to Egypt when Herod undertook the slaughter of all the male infants in the Jewish domains.

As Christian society developed through time, the status of women was constantly elevated. In modern times the values embodied in the Medieval principles and practices of chivalry are not well understood. Chivalrous treatment of women at the higher stations in society inevitably became a model for the rising middle classes and even for the humble farmers and laborers. By the standard of chivalry, women were to be honored, esteemed, respected, and loved (in the sense of agapé more so than eros). Read, if you will, the Arthurian legends, Tasso's *Jerusalem Delivered* or Ariosto's *Orlando Furioso* to get a sense of the ideals of chivalry. In modern times we have been schooled to accept as truth Cervantes' ridicule of chivalry in *Don Quixote*, rather than viewing this work in its historic context of post-Reformation efforts toward the resubordination of women.

Not only was the standing of women greatly enhanced in late-Medieval and early-Renaissance society by the notions of chivalry, but also discrete institutional developments in the church were conducive to the advancement of women. I refer particularly to the establishment of convents under

Rembrandt Van Rijn (Dutch, 1601-1669).
The Flight into Egypt: a Night Piece, c. 1651.
Etching, drypoint and burin.

the command of members of female religious orders. Abbesses and prioresses became powerful religious, social, and economic figures in this era. Let me cite a single, but emblematic, example. Trout fishing is, and as far as memory runs always has been, a quintessential male avocation. To be sure, some women in modern times have pursued this hobby, but, so it is thought, in bygone days this was a wholly masculine domain. Nothing could be further from the truth. Sir Isaac Walton's *The Complete Angler,* written in the seventeenth century, is widely regarded to be the seminal work on trout fishing. Yet it is true, and not well known, that Dame Juliana Berners, an English prioress in the fifteenth century, wrote *A Treatyse of Fysshynge wyth an Angle,* whole paragraphs, not just sentences, of which were plagiarized by Walton two centuries later.

If you want further and to me, conclusive, proof of the degree to which women had advanced before the time of the Reformation, consider for a moment the one vocation or profession that remains unattainable by women in the present progressive age. That is, of course, command of, and fighting in, combat army infantry units. Turn back to the early Renaissance. In that era we find Saint Joan of Arc fearlessly and victoriously leading French troops in the field of battle and personally engaging in combat after the male commanders had lost their will to fight. Even to this day you will find fresh flowers heaped at the foot of the gleaming statue of Saint Joan of Arc in Paris. Naturally, such an advance by a woman was not tolerated by the male power structure, and poor Saint Joan was falsely accused, tried, and executed for heresy and witchcraft.

A complex and enigmatic crisis concerning the visual and audible messages of Christianity lies at the very heart of the Reformation. Modern psychologists inform us that in communication between members of opposite sexes, women receive greater stimulation from verbal than from visual sources, while with men it is the reverse, that sight is a more vital avenue of reception than is sound.

Without doubt, the visual form of communication reigned supreme in the Medieval and Renaissance church. Cathedrals and churches presented a panorama of visual stimulation. There were stained glass windows, paintings, icons, statuary, wood carvings, metal castings, murals, frescoed ceilings, inlaid and embossed floors, illuminated manuscripts (prayer books, Bibles, hymnals), vestments, ornate reliquaries of ivory and other materials, silver communion services, and more. When the Reformation came, there was wave upon wave of destruction of these treasures by Protestant mobs (except in Germany where Luther and his followers condemned this madness and greatly curtailed it). In the Calvinist domains particularly, the decorations of the church nearly were all destroyed, and the church interiors were covered with plain whitewash. It is notable that the spasms of iconoclastic destruction surging across northern Europe had their initial focus on images of the Virgin Mary. As John Lothrop Motley recounted in his *Rise of the Dutch Republic,* when the huge image of the Virgin was carried out of the Antwerp cathedral for the annual procession on August 18, 1566, angry crowds called out, "Mayken, mayken [Little Mary], your hour has come. 'Tis your last promenade.'" The destruction of religious ornamentation, the image of the Virgin first of all, began the next day.

Priests before the Reformation had communicated in muted fashion and obscurely by muttering with their backs turned toward the congregation, in a language that only the priests understood. This was sharply changed in the Reformation. Now the focus of divine worship was upon the pastor's lengthy (hours, sometimes nearly daylong) sermon. Since the artifacts of the house of worship had been destroyed, the congregants had little choice but to receive aurally, not visually, the Christian message.

The Reformation brought about the destruction of convents. Their abbesses and prioresses were dismissed, and they and the nuns alike were often murdered. Indeed, Catherine Von Bora, the nun who later became Martin Luther's wife, would have been murdered by ravaging Protestants had she not been smuggled away in a barrel of pickled herring by a sympathetic drayman.

The reimposition of male dominance that arrived with the Reformation perhaps can best be illustrated by instances of the most extreme form of female subjugation, that of deliberate and premeditated murder. Both early and late in the course of the Reformation there are startling examples. In the beginning, Anne Boleyn, Queen of England, blameless though she was, was decapitated at the order of Henry VIII on wholly trumped up charges of treason, when the real motive for her death was to enable the king to marry another woman. At the end of the Reformation, a group of somewhat eccentric and independent women, who had done no wrong, were hanged as witches in Salem, Massachusetts.

The advancement of the status of women, linked inextricably to the ever — growing importance of the Blessed Virgin, received a huge setback in the Protestant Reformation.

SAINT JAMES, BROTHER OF CHRIST

WITH REGARD TO SAINT JAMES, our principal source of knowledge is his own epistle. In addition we have the writings of Hegesippus, who lived and wrote a little more than a century after the Crucifixion of Christ.

About the ministry and martyrdom of Saint James, Hegesippus wrote:

Together with the apostles, James our Lord's brother, succeeded to the government of the Church. He received the name of "the Just" from all men from the time of our Lord even to our own.... And alone he entered into the sanctuary and was found on his knees asking forgiveness on behalf of the people, so that his knees became hard like a camel's for he was continually bending the knee in worship to God and asking forgiveness for the people....

[T]here was an uproar among the Jews and scribes and pharisees, for they said, "There is danger that the whole people should expect Jesus as the Christ." Coming together, therefore, they said to James: "We beseech thee, restrain the people, for they are gone astray unto Jesus, imagining that he is the Christ.... Stand, therefore, upon the pinnacle of the temple, that from thy lofty station thou mayest be evident, and thy words may be easily heard by all the people." ... Therefore the aforesaid scribes and pharisees set James upon the pinnacle of the temple.... And he replied with a loud voice, "Why ask ye me of the Son of Man, since He sitteth in Heaven on the right hand of the Mighty Power, and shall come on the clouds of Heaven?" And when many were fully persuaded and gave glory at the testimony of James and said, "Hosanna to the son of David," then once more the same scribes and pharisees said among themselves: "We do ill in affording such a testimony to Jesus. Let us rather go up and cast him down, that being affrighted they may not believe him."...

And they fulfilled the scripture that is written in Isaiah: "Let us take away the just one, for he is troublesome to us. Therefore, they shall eat the fruit of their doings." Going up therefore they cast the Just One down ... And they began to stone him for the fall did not kill him. But turning he kneeled down and said: "I beseech thee, O Lord God, Father, forgive them for they know not what they do."... And one of them, a fuller, took the stick with which he beat out the clothes, and brought it down on the Just One's head. Thus was he martyred.

These events occurred about 60 AD, and are also reported by the ancient historians Clement and Eusebius. Saint James was sent to the pinnacle of the temple by the Pharisees, either as witting or unwitting agents of Satan, the same exact spot where Satan had unsuccessfully tempted his brother Jesus about 30 years ago, and Saint James yielded not to the temptations but stood firm in his faith. Recall that in the first chapter of this book, in the earliest times a brother killed his brother. But now in these later days when Christ's glory has been revealed to us, a brother gives up his own life for the sake of his brother, and as to his torturers and killers, invokes God's mercy, repeating as death approached, his own brother's precious words, "Father, forgive them for they know not what they do."

Near the beginning of the Epistle of James, the vital Christian message is stated that the rich shall be lowered and the poor will be raised up *(1:9-10)*. Familiar imagery is used to support this transition: "For the sun rises with the scorching heat and withers the grass; its flower falls, and its beauty perishes" *(1:11)*. Near the end of the epistle the rich are condemned in even stronger terms:

Come now, you rich, weep and howl for the miseries that are coming upon you. Your riches have rotted and your garments are moth-eaten. Your gold and silver have corroded, and their corrosion will be evidence against you and will eat your flesh like fire. You have laid up treasure in the last days. Behold, the wages of the laborer who mowed your fields, which you kept back by fraud, are crying out against you, and the cries of the harvesters have reached the ears of the Lord of hosts. You have lived on the earth in luxury and in self-indulgence *(5:1-5)*.

The part of the Epistle of James that has gained the greatest attention is the doctrine that faith without good works is dead. "What good is it, my brothers, if someone says he has faith but does not have works? Can that faith save him? If a brother or a sister is poorly clothed and lacking in daily food, and one of you says to them, 'Go in peace, be warmed and filled,' without giving them the things needed for the body, what good is that? So also faith by itself, if it does not have works, is dead" *(2:14-17)*.

This part of the Epistle of James seems to be directly at odds with Martin Luther's doctrine that one is justified by faith alone. The clearest statement of this is found in Article VI (II) of the *Apology*, one of the basic Lutheran charters.

Contextually, it must be remembered that Luther was angered and sickened by the perversion of good works he saw taking place in the Catholic religion. The works being urged by the church, support of monasteries and chantries, embellishment of the churches and cathedrals, and most of all, monetary payments for indulgences, went to build up the power and wealth of the church, rather than benefitting brothers and sisters in need. Understandably, Luther focused on works, as they were thus practiced, when he formulated his doctrine of justification by faith alone. Also, he was reacting very negatively to the Catholic doctrine that one is justified by works alone without regard to faith. The *Apology* makes the case that by concentrating on works, even wholesome and beneficial works, one renders superfluous the worship of Christ. The *Apology* states that obedience to basic morality and ethics can be achieved by following the prescriptions of Aristotle, Socrates, and certain other philosophers.

The doctrine of justification by faith proceeds on the belief of the certainty that a Christian will perform good works as a matter of course if he has sufficient faith. Thus Luther and his followers accept that true good works are intrinsically valuable and beneficial.

Following the Epistle of James, it does appear that commitment to both faith and good works is a reasonable way for a Christian to live. If you have faith, there is no need to reject the value of consciously doing good works as ends in themselves, rather than as spontaneous emanations from faith. If salvation comes largely or primarily from faith, the intentional doing of good works is supportive of your faith, making it easier and more certain that you will be faithful.

It is not easy to reject the teaching of the brother of Jesus that both faith and good works are worthy goals and are pathways to salvation. Remember in the preface to this book we discussed reason versus faith, and I advocated the former. Yet it seems to be true that as you build your faith, you become more able to defend Christianity in a reasoned way, and the better your reasoned defense of Christianity becomes, the firmer is your faith. In the same way, it must be true that as you do more good works, the stronger your faith be-

comes, and as your faith grows, so does your willingness and ability to perform good works build up. What we have here with faith and reason and faith and works are not downward spirals, but upward synergistic spirals of which you are drawn into the vortices. As Saint Peter wrote, "[M]ake every effort to supplement your faith with virtue, and virtue with knowledge ..."
(2 Peter 1:5).

* K. Skorecki, et al., "Y Chromosomes of Jewish Priests," *Nature* (1997); M. G. Thomas, et al., "Origins of Old Testament Priests," *Nature* (1998); M. F. Hammer, et al., "Extended Y Chromosome Haplotypes Resolve Multiple and Unique Lineages of the Jewish Priesthood," *Human Genetics* (2009).

** D. M. Behar, et al., "The Matrilineal Ancestry of Ashkenazi Jewry: Portrait of a Recent Founder Event," *American Journal of Human Genetics* (2006).

*** G. Atzmon, et al., "Abraham's Children in the Genome Era: Major Jewish Diaspora Populations Comprise Distinct Genetic Clusters with Shared Middle Eastern Ancestry," *American Journal of Human Genetics* (2010); N. M. Kopelman, "Genomic Microsatellites Identity Shared Jewish Ancestry Intermediate Between Middle Eastern and European Populations," B*MC Genetics* (2009); A. Nebel, "The Y Chromosome Pool of Jews as Part of the Genetic Landscape of the Middle East," *American Journal of Human Genetics* (2001).

Chapter Nine
Saint Paul

CHRISTIANITY IN RECENT YEARS has lost a measure of credibility in consequence of Saint Paul's epistolary pronouncements that wives must be subordinate to their husbands and women must not occupy positions of leadership in the church. The purpose of this discussion of Saint Paul's writings is to seek enlightenment about the legitimacy or illegitimacy of the apparent Pauline anti-feminism.

As a member of the Missouri Synod Lutheran Church, I accept the doctrine of Biblical inerrancy. The beginning of our analysis requires an explanation of the concept of inerrancy as applied to the epistles of Saint Paul. We are quick to assert the inerrancy of the Gospels, the Torah, and the Old Testament historical books. There is no reason to say the prophetic books are not inerrant, only that we must be cautious with them and not treat our own understandings or interpretations of the prophecies as inerrant, except when the prophecies have been plainly fulfilled, most notably with the birth, ministry, crucifixion, Resurrection, and Ascension of our Lord.

The application of the principle of inerrancy to the Pauline epistles is particularly complex since Saint Paul himself confessed his own errancy, and the epistles themselves contain quite apparent contradictions. First let us look at Saint Paul's own confession. Just near the end of the greatest tribute to love ever written, in the Thirteenth Chapter of First Corinthians, comes the admission of errancy. I quote from the early translation, the Geneva Bible, where the passage (verse 12) is much more powerful and majestic than in modern translations:

> For now we see through a glasse darke-in: but then shall we see face to face. Now I knowe in part: but then shall I knowe [fully] as I am knowen.

Saint Paul acknowledges that not just you and I do not see, appreciate, and understand the full Christian message, but by using the word "we," he acknowledges that he also possesses these same limitations which shall not be removed until after death, when we come into God's presence. Saint Paul states his own limitations even more bluntly in *2 Corinthians 12:11,* where he says, "I have been a fool!" Saint Peter also acknowledged Saint Paul's fallibility when he wrote, "There are some things in them [Saint Paul's epistles] that are hard to understand, . . ." *(2 Peter 3:15).*

Therefore inerrancy, when applied to the Pauline epistles, requires acceptance of the fact that they contain errors. A belief in inerrancy, when applied to the letters of Saint Paul, means rather a belief in their errancy. This approach, if too freely applied, however, would lead to a deconstruction and debasement of these vital canonical texts. A suggestion is made at the end of this discussion of how we may narrowly and cautiously apply the concept of errancy to Saint Paul's writings.

Christianity owes an enormous debt to Saint Paul. Hardly any of us would be Christians today had he not propagated the faith to the Gentiles. Nevertheless, Saint Paul was not divine and was subject to self-confessed human fallibility. Indeed, the sufferings that Saint Paul experienced surely must have had an impact on his thought processes, human as he was, that could have led him into error, for he was imprisoned multiple times (at least four of the epistles being written in prison), five times received 39 lashes by the Jews, three times was whipped by the Romans, was stoned once, experienced three shipwrecks, was frequently deprived of sleep, food, clothing, and shelter, was once under sentence of death, and suffered a painful physical ailment from which he was never relieved *(2 Corinthians 11:23-27, 12:7-9; 2 Timothy 4:17; Ephesians 6:20; Philippians 1:7; Colossians 4:10; and Philemon 1:1).*

Saint Paul was not a firsthand witness of Christ's ministry, but depended for his information on a period of study for two weeks with Saint Peter and briefly with Saint James the Younger *(Galatians 1:18-19).* Saint Paul stated that he knew no other Apostles, but elsewhere he acknowledged meeting Saint John, as well *(Galatians 2:9).* He also worked closely with the two non-disciple Gospel writers, Saint Mark and Saint Luke, in nurturing the Gentile churches and most likely learned fully from them the contents of their Gospels *(2 Timothy 4:11).*

Before proceeding to the analysis of Saint Paul's opinions about women, it would be helpful to examine briefly his views on a distinctly unequal human relationship, the institution of slavery. Slave masters in the pre-Civil War

South took much solace from Saint Paul's defenses of slavery. Slaves are told repeatedly to obey their masters (*Ephesians 6:5; Titus 2:19*). Yet no honest interpreter of the Gospels could ever conclude that Jesus blessed slavery. To the contrary, He told us that we must be servants, not masters, just as He Himself took "the form of a servant" (*Philippians 2:7*). Elsewhere in the epistles, Saint Paul made statements plainly opposed to slavery. He wrote that if a slave had a chance to become free, he should do so (*1 Corinthians 7:21*). Twice he wrote that there is no distinction between enslaved and free (*Galatians 3:28 and Colossians 3:11*). Finally, in the beautiful and tender letter to Philemon (verse 16), he made the point that the Philemon's slave, Onesimus, now that he had converted to Christianity, was his dear brother in Christ, a relationship plainly incompatible with slavery.

Slavery and the subordination of women were prevalent social conditions in the Roman Empire of Saint Paul's time. His great mission was to propagate the faith. Christianity itself necessarily rejected many prevailing social norms. It was Saint Paul's strategy not to challenge existing patterns of conduct more than minimally necessary to accommodate the expansion of the Christian faith. Thus, he plainly called upon his followers to obey the civil authorities and abide by the laws (*Romans 13:1-2*). *

Before proceeding to a discussion of Saint Paul's statements concerning duties of husbands and wives, it is helpful to consider Saint Paul's own preferences regarding marriage. Saint Paul made it clear that for himself, he preferred celibacy, not marriage (*1 Corinthians 7:1, 7, 26, 28, 32-34, 37-38*). While it would be useless to speculate about Saint Paul's sexual orientation, his own election of celibacy has at least some significance for his capacity to give correct marital advice, just as we Lutherans believe it to be much more useful to seek marital counseling from a married pastor, than from a celibate priest. Surely one who is celibate and without desire to be married has less of an understanding and appreciation, than a married clergyman, of the practical issues that arise in the course of a marriage.

Just as was the case with addressing slavery, Saint Paul wrote inconsistently regarding female independence. In his very first reference to the issue, Saint Paul wrote that the wife is the master of the husband's body, just as the husband is the master of the wife's body (*1 Corinthians 7:4*). This phraseology implies a standoff or a potentially irreconcilable conflict between spouses in the event of disagreement. Also in the same passage of Galatians cited above for no distinction between enslaved and free, Saint Paul also made the point that there is no difference between men and women, that all are one in union with Christ (*Galatians 3:28*).

The first statement by Saint Paul on the subordination of women to their husbands occurs in *1 Corinthians 11:3, 8-9*, but verse 16 indicates that this is not Saint Paul's pronouncement, but rather a fact of prevailing social practice. The unmistakable Pauline pronouncements of the duty of wives to submit to their husbands are found in *Ephesians 5:22-24, Colossians 3:18*, and *Titus 2:6*. But even these edicts are tempered by the further explanation that a man's duty to his wife is not to exercise unbridled control over her, but rather to love her just as much as Christ loved the church and gave His life for it, and to love her as much as he loves his own body (*Ephesians 5:25, 28; Colossians 3:19*).

It is useful to consider the respective powers and obligations of spouses to one another in the context of contemporary institutions and norms of marriage. Jewish husbands were free to divorce their wives instantaneously and without any ground whatsoever. Among the Gentiles it was widely accepted for males to have multiple wives. Even the Romans themselves had come to debase marriage, so that both adultery and divorce were widely practiced and tolerated. Truly, Christianity brought about a fundamental change with the introduction of the gold standard of lifetime monogamous marriage, with divorce allowed only on account of adultery by the other spouse *(Matthew 19:9)*. This development was enormously empowering to women. Their husbands were no longer free to put them aside (as long as the wives abstained from adultery), and of great importance, the wives, and their children were given the assurance of continuing support and sustenance.

Monogamous marriage did not instantly become the norm in Christian communities, for Saint Paul repeatedly exhorted that, whatever may be the marital condition of ordinary church members, church leaders, helpers, and elders, must have only one wife *(1 Timothy 3:2, 12; Titus 2:6)*.

It is unfortunate that we have only the letters from Saint Paul, not the letters to him from struggling Christian congregations, reciting the problems, dilemmas, and obstacles that they faced in trying to engraft Christian ethics and morality into diverse existing cultures. Let us imagine (not a far-fetched idea) that the church at Ephesus or Colossus wrote to complain of how wives, with their newfound rights in Christian marriage, had begun to assert themselves as the superior or stronger member of the marital union. Was it in response to such concerns that Saint Paul wrote the advice that women must submit themselves to their husbands? Perhaps Saint Paul had hoped the pronouncements would lead to fully equal states of disagreement, the wives claiming the great powers granted to them in Saint Matthew's Gospel and the husbands relying on Saint Paul's admonitions of the duty of wifely obedience. Surely Saint Paul knew, and expected his flocks would discover, that the resolution of such seeming irreconcilability would be for a husband and wife to join hands, to fall on their knees before God, and to pray for His guidance in preserving their union, thus ending the animosity and misunderstanding into which they had fallen. Put simply, true appreciation of the Gospel principles of forgiveness, tolerance, unselfishness, servanthood, and, above all, love ("Love is patient and kind; love does not envy or boast; it is not arrogant or rude; it does not insist on its own way; it is not irritable or resentful . . ." *1 Corinthians 13:4)*, soon enough will melt away the bad feelings and disagreements that develop between husbands and wives. To end all doubt about this, Saint Paul not only told wives to submit to their husbands, but also told husbands to love their wives so much as to be willing to give their own lives for them *(Ephesians 5:22-25, 28)*.

When it comes to the woman's role in church leadership, there is no inconsistency in Saint Paul's statements. Rather, there is a blatant contradiction between what he advocated and what he himself practiced. If ever the admonition, "Do as I say, not as I do," had a hollow ring, it was with regard to Saint Paul's actual practices concerning women's positions in the church. What Saint Paul said on the subject was clear enough: women should not speak in church *(1 Corinthians 14:34-35)*, and he, Paul, does not allow women to teach or to have authority over men *(1 Timothy 2:12)*. Yet Paul repeatedly acknowledged women in church leadership roles: Prisca *(1 Corinthians 16:19)*; Euodia and Syntyche *(Philippians 4:2-3)*; Phoebe, Mary, and Junia *(Romans 16:1, 3, 6, 7)*.

Considerable insight into Saint Paul's thinking on the subject is gained from his explanation of why women should not be heard in church, as being based on Jewish law *(1 Corinthians 14:34-35)*. This makes no sense. The central message of Galatians is that Christians must adhere to their faith rather than be blindly obedient to the law, and that where faith and law are in conflict, faith must prevail. By contrast, with yielding to Jewish law on the muzzling of women, Saint Paul made it clear that circumcision, a central feature of Jewish law, had no relevance for Christians *(1 Corinthians 7:18-19)* and was much apposed by him *(Galatians 5:2-3)*. Perhaps the best explanation for Saint Paul's negative views on female church leadership can be found in his general preference, previously discussed, not to displace prevailing social norms unless necessitated by the Christian faith. In other words, he must have concluded that the negative effect on church development from empowering women justified their exclusion from leadership roles.

The ultimate question we have is: With what freedom may we reject a pronouncement by Saint Paul in the epistles? I suggest that we should never prefer our own ideas over those of Saint Paul, unless he has made contradictory statements on the subject, or unless his words have diverged from his actual practices. I have been able to identify only three subjects on which there are such divergences: namely, slavery, wives' duties to husbands, and women's role in the church. Thus, we can legitimately claim the right to reject a teaching of Saint Paul on only a very few points.

In order to decide which contradictory position of Saint Paul's to accept, I suggest that there be a twofold analysis: first, the guidance on the subject that is to be derived from the Gospels, those quintessentially inerrant parts of the Bible, and second, the understanding to be gained from examining relevant historical circumstances.

We have already concluded that freedom, not slavery, is supported by the Gospels. Similarly, we must conclude that freedom and equality of women are supported by the Gospels. The Gospels in no way suggest that women are not to be equal partners in marriage, or that they cannot occupy leadership positions in the church. Indeed, women appear in a far more favorable light than men at the very time of Christ's crucifixion. Not only did Saint Peter deny his affiliation with Christ three times, but all the male Disciples, save for Saint John the Evangelist, disappeared from sight as Christ underwent his suffering and death. By contrast, the women, the Blessed Virgin, Saint Mary Magdalene, the other Saint Mary, and Saint Martha, were with Jesus every step of the way while He bore the cross, and remained with Him until He died on the cross.

Finally, an examination of relevant historical circumstances reveals general submission of women and domination by men in the institution of marriage, except in the Christian community, and the preclusion of women from leading in Jewish worship, but the acceptance of female church leadership by none other than Saint Paul himself.

The conclusions, to our inquiry to which we are irresistibly drawn, are that marriage should be an equal partnership between wife and husband, and no position of church leadership should be denied to women. We are fully free to disregard Saint Paul's pronouncements in these matters.

*St. Paul's preoccupation with guarding and expanding the fragile early Christian churches at the expense of yielding his beliefs on non-essential points is captured in *1 Corinthians 9:20–22*: "To the Jews I became as a Jew, in order to win Jews. To those under the law I became as one under the law (though not being myself under the law) that I might win those under the law. To those outside of the law I became as one outside the law (not being outside the law of God but under the law of Christ) that I might win those outside the law. To the weak, I became weak, that I might win the weak. I have become all things to all people, that by all means I might save some."

Chapter Ten
HOLY TRINITY

FOR 39 YEARS MY WIFE GAY AND I attended Holy Trinity Episcopal Church in Greensboro, North Carolina. She was an observant, although not devout, Episcopalian, while for all but the last three of those years, I was a Unitarian and would neither say the creed nor take communion. Our children were baptized, confirmed, and married there. Gay's funeral took place there. Holy Trinity contains hundreds of remarkable wood carvings lovingly made by members of the congregation in the 1940's, the most splendid of which is an amazingly intricate carving of the Last Supper on the altar of the chapel.

In 1971, we bought a farm and later another farm and then a third farm in mountainous Ashe County, North Carolina. On weekends and vacations, we involved the children in herding cattle — that primordial occupation that has ancient connections to modern democratic freedom *(see page 2)* — and associated tasks of raising, drying, and grinding field corn; fence building (from hand split black locust posts); barn building; and cutting, raking, forking, and carrying hay to the barn, all in the old fashioned way. We gardened, grew apples and other fruit, and made and fermented cider.

Occasionally, our family attended another Holy Trinity Episcopal Church, the site of a magnificent fresco of the Last Supper, not many miles away from the farm. Now that Gay is gone, in my old age I have given the farms to my three daughters. While I disagree with some of their practices of husbandry or the lack thereof, I maintain tactful silence, and instead take enormous pleasure in seeing grandchildren engaging in the same games, amusements, and tasks that occupied their parents as youngsters so many years ago.

Shouldn't there be a third Holy Trinity Episcopal Church in this series? There is! The formal name of the American Cathedral (Episcopal) in Paris is Holy Trinity. The altar of this cathedral is decorated with a triptych depicting the Crucifixion. (Note the relationship of the two Last Suppers and the Crucifixion, page 92). This third Holy Trinity is the site of my marriage to Carolyn in the year 2012. She had been my friend and Gay's friend for 45 years. Her husband Jim was the godfather of my only son.

THE HOLY TRINITY
IN THE OLD TESTAMENT

*T*HE DUTY OF WORSHIP AND GLORIFICATION of the Son and Holy Spirit is only implicit in the New Testament *(see pages 56–59)*, and was not fully formalized until three centuries after Christ's death. Yet the markers, precursors, and suggestions of the glorification of the Triune God are found throughout the Holy Bible.

The Old Testament declares the power, majesty, and dominion of God the Father: "The Lord our God, the Lord is one. You shall love the Lord your God with all your heart and with all your soul and with all your might" *(Deuteronomy 6:4-5)*. It is perhaps upon this ringing declaration that most unitarian doctrines down through the ages have been founded. Yet there are equally compelling; scriptural pronouncements that God the Son and God the Holy Spirit have been with us for all time.

Saint John's Gospel begins with the unforgettable lines, that Saint Athanasius records, that were essential to the defeat of the Arian (primitive Unitarian) heresy: "In the beginning was the Word and the Word was with God, and the Word was God. . . . And the Word became flesh and dwelt among us, and we have seen his glory, glory as of the only Son from the Father, . . ." *(John 1:1-2, 14)*. *Daniel 7:13-14* explicitly refers to God the Son: "I saw in the night vision. And behold, with the clouds of heaven there came one like a son of man, and he came to the Ancient of Days and was presented before him. And to him was given dominion and glory and a kingdom, that all people, nations and languages should serve him; his dominion is an everlasting dominion, which shall not pass away, and his kingdom is one that shall not be destroyed." Other Old Testament references to God the Son include *Genesis 16:7-14, 21:17-18, 22:9-18, 28:10-22* and *32:22-32; Exodus 13:21* and *23:20-22; Numbers 22:21-41; Judges 2:1-5, 6:7-24* and *13:3-22; 2 Samuel 24:16; Psalm 2, 7, and 110:1; Isaiah 7:14, 9:6,* and *63:9; Jeremiah 23:5-6; Proverbs 30:4; Zechariah 1:10-11* and *12:8;* and *Malachi 3:1.*

Genesis states that, "In the beginning God created the heavens and the earth. The earth was without form and void, and darkness was over the face of the deep. And the Spirit of God was hovering over the face of the waters"

(Genesis 1:1-2). Other Old Testament references to God the Holy Spirit are found in *Nehemiah 9:20; Job 26:13* and *33:4; Psalm 104:30, 106:32-33, 139:1-24,* and *143:10; 2 Samuel 23:1-3; Isaiah 11:2* and *40:13; Ezekiel 11:5;* and *Micah 2:7.*

The references to God in three persons are manifold throughout the Old Testament. God refers to Himself in the plural form in many verses, for example *Genesis 1:26, 2:18, 3:22, 1 and 1:7-9.* A number of verses refer to the plural faces, persons or presences of God, for example *Exodus 33:14, Deuteronomy 4:37,* and *Job 13:8.*

In Isaiah we find an explicit reference to the Triune God of Father, Son, and Holy Spirit: "Draw near to me, hear this: from the beginning I have not spoken in secret, from the time it came to be I have been there. And now the *Lord God* has sent *me,* and *his Spirit*" *(Isaiah 48:16).*

In many and various ways, God in the Old Testament prepared His people for the manifestation of the Holy Trinity. Perhaps the Trinitarian precursors with the most engaging imagery are the appearance of the three angels to Abraham and the imperishability of the three men cast into the fiery furnace.

Genesis 18:1-14 reports the visit of the three angels. First, the text states that the Lord appeared to him; next, it says that there were three men standing in front of him. Although Abraham saw there were three, he addressed them first as "O Lord," but then as "yourselves." Concerning the annunciation of Sarah's pregnancy and birthing in her elderly and childless state, at first "they" spoke to Abraham, but then "the Lord" spoke.

Childbirth was forecast similarly in the old age of Elizabeth, who bore John the Baptist, cousin and baptizer of our Lord and Savior, and was "filled with the Holy Spirit even from his mother's womb" *(Luke 1:11-15).*

Shadrach, Meshach, and Abednego had been made administrators of Babylon, but they refused Nebuchadnezzar's order to fall down and worship a golden image. Nebuchadnezzar in a fury ordered that his fiery furnace be made seven times hotter than usual and that the three Jewish men be bound and cast into it. Although the heat was so intense it killed those who cast the men into the furnace, Shadrach, Meshach, and Abednego emerged unharmed without as much as a hair of their heads being singed *(Daniel 2-4).* See the image of the three men in the fiery furnace in the *Appendix (page 227).* This event symbolized the imperishability of the Holy Trinity and the ability of the

Josse Lieferinxe (South Netherlandish,
Active 1493–1503/08)
Abraham Visited by the Three Angels
Oil on wood panel
DENVER ART MUSEUM

Triune God to pass unscathed even through Satan's flaming domain ("Christ
. . . was not abandoned to Hades. . . ." *Acts 2:31).*

Proto-Trinitarian references in the Old Testament are too numerous to
recount. Some of these include:

- The three feasts, Unleavened Bread, Weeks and Tabernacle
  (Deuteronomy 16:16).
- The three animals, heifer, she-goat and ram, each three years old, of
  the divine seal of God's covenant with Abraham *(Genesis 15:9).*
- The three spies who went into the Promised Land and found grapes,
  figs, and pomegranates *(Numbers 13:23).*
- The threefold division of the Old Testament into law, prophets, and
  psalms *(Luke 24:44).*
- The divine judgment against Belshazzar: Mene (God has numbered
  your kingdom), Tekel (you are weighed in the balance and found

wanting), Peres (your kingdom is divided and given to the Medes and Persians) *(Daniel 5:25-28)*.

  ℝ The cry of the seraphim: "Holy, holy, holy is the Lord of hosts" *(Isaiah 6:3)*.

For those of us who believe in Biblical inerrancy *(see page 17)*, the Trinitarian threefold corruption of God's Word by Eve that led to the Fall holds particular meaning. We are enjoined not to take from, add to, or alter God's Word. Eve did all three. God had said, "You may surely [or freely] eat of every tree of the garden, but of the tree of the knowledge of good and evil you shall not eat, for in the day that you eat of it you shall surely die" *(Genesis 2:16-17)*. Eve corrupted God's words and said to Satan, "We may eat of the fruit of the trees in the garden, but God said, 'You shall not eat of the fruit of the tree that is in the midst of the garden, neither shall you touch it lest you die'" *(Genesis 3:2-3)*. First, Eve *omitted* the word surely or freely, making God appear less bountiful than He was. Second, Eve *added* the words "neither shall you touch it," making God seem more severe than He was. Third, Eve *altered* the words "you shall surely die" to be "lest you die," weakening the certainty of divine retribution.

THE TRANSFIGURATION AS A TRINITARIAN STATEMENT

*I*N THE TRANSFIGURATION, which is recorded in the Synoptic Gospels *(Matthew 17:1-13, Mark 9:2-13, Luke 9:28-36)*, Jesus took Saint Peter, Saint John the Evangelist, and Saint James the Elder with him to Mt. Tabor. Jesus was transfigured, so that His face was like the sun and His clothes became white as light. Moses and Elijah appeared, talking with Jesus. God the Father spoke, saying, "This is my beloved Son with whom I am well pleased; listen to him" *(Matthew 17:5)*. Moses and Elijah disappeared, and Jesus was alone. Jesus told the three Disciples not to tell anyone what had occurred.

Saint Peter offered to build three tents, one each for Jesus, Moses, and Elijah, but there was no response to this suggestion, since he had failed to understand that the Transfiguration was not an invitation to worship and glorify Moses and Elijah along with Christ, but rather was another precursor of the Holy Trinity. Moses and Elijah represented the law and the prophets, and of course, Christ Himself stood for the redemptive love and sacrifice of the

Gospel. The disappearance of Moses and Elijah with Christ alone remaining, symbolized the triumph and transcendency of the Gospel.

God the Father appeared on only one other occasion in the New Testament, at Christ's Baptism, where He made a similar statement of being well pleased with His Son *(Matthew 3:17, Mark 1:11, Luke 3:22)*. God the Father had spoken over and over again in the Old Testament to Abraham, to Moses, to many leaders in the historical books, and to many of the prophets. Now He had chosen to speak instead only through His Son. And Jesus did speak, in pages and pages of the Gospel texts, often conveniently printed for us in red ink. The Gospels contained a complete account of Christ's essential words during His ministry. His words were committed first to memory and soon after in the written Gospels. Then it was no longer necessary for either God the Father or God the Son to speak again, and neither did speak, except after the

Giovanni Bellini
Transfiguration (1518–1520)
Oil on wood panel
Naples, Museo di Capodimonte

Ascension, when Jesus appeared to Saint Paul to bring about his conversion.

God the Holy Spirit appears at critical times in the Gospels. The Holy Spirit is the means by which the Blessed Virgin becomes impregnated *(Luke 1:35)*, and the Holy Spirit descends like a dove upon Jesus at His Baptism, *(Matthew 3:16, Mark 1:10, Luke 3:22)*. In Saint John's Gospel, Christ informs us that He will leave behind the Holy Spirit, for us as a "Helper" and as the "Spirit of Truth," *(John 14:16-17, 16:7-13)*.

The New Testament nowhere expressly commands the worship and glorification of God the Son and God the Holy Spirit *(see pages 56–59)*. This is implicit, not explicit, in the Gospels. To learn why Jesus Christ and the Holy Spirit become part of the Triune God, it is necessary to examine the history of the first three centuries of Christianity. Before doing that, however, certain other precursors of the Holy Trinity need to be considered.

At the Transfiguration, not merely the three central figures — Christ, Moses and Elijah — were proto-Trinitarian, but so were the three witnesses, Saints Peter, John and James the Elder, particularly when the vital role of each in forming, advancing, and protecting the church is taken into account. These same witnesses were present by themselves with Christ on three occasions. In addition to the Transfiguration, these three accompanied Jesus to the garden of Gethsemane *(Matthew 26:36-41)* and at the raising from the dead of the synagogue ruler's daughter *(Mark 5:35-43)*.

Saint Peter was the first of the Disciples to be called by Jesus *(Matthew 4:18)*. Saint Peter was the rock upon which Christ chose to build the church. Jesus asked, "[W]ho do you say I am?" Peter replied, "You are the Christ, the Son of the living God." Jesus answered, "Blessed are you Simon Bar Jonah! ... [Y]ou are Peter, and on this rock, I will build my church, and the gates of hell shall not prevail against it. I will give you the keys of Heaven" *(Matthew 16:15-19)*. Jesus left the members of the Christian church in Saint Peter's keeping when, not long before the Ascension, He three times enjoined Peter: "Feed my lambs. . . . Tend my sheep. . . . Feed my sheep" *(John 21:15-17)*.

Saints John and James the Elder are named by Jesus as "Sons of Thunder" in *Mark 3:17*. A permissive alternative translation is "Sons of Thunderer." To the hearers and readers of the Gospel in the Greco-Roman world, this label would have had great significance, for the king of the gods, Zeus or Jupiter, was commonly referred to as the Thunderer, the one who formed and dispatched thunder and lightening. To call these disciples "Sons of Thunderer" would suggest that they were directly descended from God the Father. Of course, the Christians of Jewish extraction would have been less moved by this reference since they already knew that everyone is a child of God (". . . Adam, the son of God." *Luke 3:38*).

Saint John is immensely important to the Christian faith. After Saint Peter denied three times being a follower of Christ *(John 18:17, 25-26)*, all the Disciples fled the approaching Crucifixion, except John, and he remained with Jesus every step of the way and to His death on the cross *(John 19:26)*. Saint John wrote the Gospel which stands out above all the others in its spiritual richness and analytical power. He wrote three magnificent Epistles, which emphasize properties of love *(1 John 2:9, 10, 3:11-18, 4:2-12)* and truth *(1 John 3:19* and *2 John 4)*, that become critical to the understanding of the Holy Trinity *(see pages 95–97)*. In his old age, after all the other Disciples had been martyred, Saint John retired to the Island of Patmos, where he recorded the Book of Revelation. *(For a further discussion of Saint John, see Chapter Seven.)*

But what of Saint James the Elder? His activities recounted in the Gospels are minimal. With his brother Saint John, he offered to command fire to come down from heaven (as one might expect from the Sons of Thunderer) to consume the Samaritans, who had refused food and lodging to Jesus as He passed through their land, but Jesus declined the offer and rebuked them *(Luke 9:54-55)*. As we shall see, Saint James' offer of violence to support the cause of Christianity was a precursor of his bloody intervention against Muslim invaders eight centuries later. The only other Scriptural reference to Saint James the Elder is when he and Saint John asked to be seated immediately to the left and right of Jesus in the heavenly kingdom, but Jesus declined by saying that was a decision reserved to God the Father *(Matthew 20:20-23, Mark 10:35-41)*.

The greatest actions of Saint James the Elder were post-Scriptural. Those of us who are Protestants must strive to put aside our prejudices and not be Pharisaic *(see Chapter Three)*. Recall that the occurrence of miracles with some frequency can hardly be denied rationally *(see pages 23–25)*. The annals of the Catholic Church record multitudinous apparitions of various saints, the Blessed Virgin, and even Jesus Christ. To deny all of these would require a belief that the tens of thousands of witnesses were liars or suffered from hal-

Francisco Pacheco(?)
St. James the Greater Conquering the Moors (c. 1625)
Tempera and gold leaf on vellum
(from patent deed of Philip IV to Vicom Monroi)
PRIVATE COLLECTION

lucinations — hardly a rational position. We Protestants, who do not reject the central teachings of the New Testament, are bound to accept at least one apparition of the risen Christ, the one recorded in *Acts 9:4-6,* where He brings about the conversion of Saint Paul. Saint James the Elder was the first of the Disciples to be martyred *(Acts 12:2)*.

By the mid-ninth century, Islam had wiped out Christianity across much of the globe, leaving the conquered Christians faced with two options: conversion or death. Asian Christian congregations all the way from the Eastern Mediterranean to Western China had been destroyed. The Christian churches of North Africa almost all had been wiped out. Muslim armies were swarming across Spain, victorious everywhere, and all of Europe was imperiled. The very survival of the Christian faith was at stake. At the battle of Clavijo in 844, the vastly outnumbered and demoralized Christian forces turned the tide against the Muslim hordes when Saint James the Elder was seen by thousands in a full suit of armor riding on a galloping white horse with a sword in one hand and the banner of victory in the other, slaughtering great numbers of Muslims and inspiring their army to surrender.

He came to the assistance of the Christian forces at least forty times during that period. The Muslim advance was halted. The armed struggle in Europe between Christians and Muslims was largely confined to the Iberian Peninsula, and the Muslims were driven out finally in 1492. These events were recorded over and over again in letters, journals, and other writings, some of which remain in the archives of the Catholic Church.

The site of the grave of Saint James the Elder at Santiago de Compostela in Spain remains perhaps the most visited pilgrim shrine in the world to this day. If all Christendom is again in grave danger, will the Lord God once again send Saint James to help us? I would not count it out.

THE HOLY TRINITY
IN THE EARLY CHRISTIAN CHURCH

Saint matthew's gospel ends with Jesus' great commission to His Disciples to minister to all nations, "baptizing them in the name of the Father and of the Son and of the Holy Spirit" *(Matthew 28:19)*. From the earliest times, baptism was carried out in these Trinitarian terms. The baptismal ceremony from ancient days also enjoined the parents and supporters of the baptismal candidate to help protect the child from an evil trinity: the world, the flesh, and the devil. For those of you who do not fully appreciate how corrosive and injurious are the forces of the world, the flesh, and the devil, not only imperiling to eternal salvation, but also harmful in this earthly life, you need only watch DVDs of a trilogy of operas, Handel's *Giulio Cesare* (the world), Mozart's *Don Giovanni* (the flesh) and Gounod's *Faust* (the devil).

The first, second, and third century Christian church faced immense dangers, from both within and without, that placed its very existence in doubt.

From within, the church was wracked by heresies. Some of these are discussed in Chapter Seven, including the Manichean that featured nature worship, Gnosticism that sought to intellectualize and universalize the faith and deprive it of its spiritual force and the personal connectivity to God, tendencies for Christianity to become a minor Jewish sect, efforts at causing Christianity to become polytheistic in a manner similar to the Greco-Roman pantheon, and above all, a series of movements to deny the divinity of Christ or to regard him as a lesser and inferior deity, and to move into a kind of Unitarianism. The final and most threatening of these movements was Arianism.

From without, the church was constantly under persecution. Not only did the seven great persecutions take place over time, but as part of its daily life, the early Christian church was also constantly subjected to deadly coercive measures aimed at eliminating the faith *(see page 54)*.

For Christianity to withstand these immense interior and exterior pressures, it was necessary for the church to turn to form and definition of the greatest potency and persistency.

The number three has long been known to possess intrinsically supreme powers. In music, three is the basic perfect meter. It is by no means happenstance that many of the great Christian choral works feature prominently the meter three, including Bach's *Christmas Oratorio, St. Matthew Passion,* and *St. John Passion,* Handel's *Messiah* and *Joshua,* Haydn's *Creation,* and Brahms's *German Requiem.*

In rhetoric, a series of three related, but distinct words has long been known to be the most readily remembered and most easily absorbed. Consider the Lord's prayer, the prayer prescribed by Christ Himself, which ascribes all *kingdom, power,* and *glory* to God. Another example, as noted above, is the baptismal creed's rejection of the *world*, the *flesh*, and the *devil*. Yet another example is in the *Apology* written by the theologian Justin Martyr in about 150 AD, "Christ who appeared for our sake, *body, reason* and *soul*." A further example is in Saint Paul's great discourse on love in *1 Corinthians 13:13*, "So now *faith*, *hope*, and *love* abide, these three; but the greatest of these is love." Many examples may be drawn from Revelation, which is replete with such trilogies, the following from the Prologue alone: Blessed are those who *read* aloud, who *hear*, and who *keep* what is written *(1:3)*; the Divine Being which *was*, and which *is*, and which *is to come (1:4)*; Christ as the faithful *witness*, the *firstborn* of the dead, and the *ruler* of kings on earth *(1:5)*. Secular examples of three linked words are also abundant, for example, from our own Declaration of Independence the rights of life, liberty, and the pursuit of happiness, and the French Revolutionary motto of liberty, equality, and fraternity.

The ministry of Jesus in and of itself was not only proto-Trinitarian, but also in its threesomeness inseparably linked to the Eucharist. *(See the discussion of the three Holy Trinity churches on page 81)*. From the Gospel of Saint John the Evangelist we learn that the three-year ministry of Christ was marked by three annual Passovers:

- Passover One in and around Cana in 28 AD, where and about when the first miracle of our Lord took place: the transformation of water into wine *(John 2:1-13)*;
- Passover Two on a mountain near the Sea of Galilee in 29 AD, when and where He miraculously fed the five thousand with five loaves of bread and two fish *(John 6:1-13)*; and
- Passover Three in our Savior's thirty-third year at Golgotha in 30 AD, where on the Preparation Day of the Passover he was crucified *(John 19:14-23)*.

Truly can we Christians say, as many of us do to this day in our weekly Eucharistic feast, "Christ, our Passover, is sacrificed for us." The night before the Crucifixion, our Savior at the Last Supper told the Disciples that the bread was His body, "Take, eat; this is my body;" and the wine was His blood, "Drink from it, all of you, for this is my blood of the covenant" *(Matthew 26:26-28)*. The wine Jesus at Passover One had miraculously created from water now became, and for us Christians at every Eucharistic celebration becomes, miraculously transformed into Christ's blood at the Third Passover. The bread that Jesus at Passover Two had miraculously multiplied to feed the thousands became, and for us Christians at every Eucharistic celebration becomes, miraculously transformed into Christ's body at the Third Passover.

Undoubtedly as a consequence of the many Scriptural proto-Trinitarian images and references, the early church fathers soon recognized the essentiality of glorifying and worshiping God the Father, God the Son, and God the Holy Spirit as the Triune Deity. Between 174 and 189 AD, the theologian Irenaeus of Lyons wrote in *Against the Heresies*, "the faith in one God the Father Almighty, Creator of heaven and earth . . .; and in one Jesus Christ, the Son of God, who was enfleshed for our salvation, and in the Holy Spirit. . . ." The theologian Hippolytus in *Contra Noetum* about the turn of the second century wrote, "Scriptures . . . have to be investigated, to see how they speak of the Father, Son and Holy Spirit, so that we might believe in the Father, glorify the Son and receive the Spirit . . . ." Such writings as these obviously made up the body of dogma from which Saint Athanasius, writing for the Council of Nicea, formalized as the Nicene Creed. Athanasius is credited, after a long and essentially non-violent struggle, with overcoming the Arian heresy, the most powerful of the ancient primitive Unitarianisms. In order to make clear, plain, and undebatable the doctrine of the Holy Trinity, Saint Athanasius wrote the creed named for him, which my own Lutheran Church recites in full once a year during mass:

THE CREED OF ATHANASIUS
Written against the Arians.

Whoever desires to be saved must, above all, hold the catholic faith.

Whoever does not keep it whole and undefiled will without doubt perish eternally.

And the catholic faith is this,

that we worship one God in Trinity and Trinity in unity, neither confusing the persons nor dividing the substance.

For the Father is one person, the Son is another, and the Holy Spirit is another.

But the Godhead of the Father and of the Son and of the Holy Spirit is one: the glory equal, the majesty coeternal.

Such as the Father is, such is the Son, and such is the Holy Spirit:

the Father uncreated, the Son uncreated, the Holy Spirit uncreated;

the Father infinite, the Son infinite, the Holy Spirit infinite;

the Father eternal, the Son eternal, the Holy Spirit eternal.

And yet there are not three Eternals, but one Eternal,

just as there are not three Uncreated or three Infinites, but one Uncreated and one Infinite.

In the same way, the Father is almighty, the Son almighty, the Holy Spirit almighty;

and yet there are not three Almighties but one Almighty.

So the Father is God, the Son is God, the Holy Spirit is God;

and yet there are not three Gods, but one God.

So the Father is Lord, the Son is Lord, the Holy Spirit is Lord;

and yet there are not three Lords, but one Lord.

Just as we are compelled by the Christian truth to acknowledge each distinct person as God and Lord,

so also are we prohibited by the catholic religion to say that there are three Gods or Lords.

The Father is not made nor created nor begotten by anyone. The Son is neither made nor created, but begotten of the Father alone.

The Holy Spirit is of the Father and of the Son, neither made nor created nor begotten but proceeding.

Thus, there is one Father, not three Fathers; one Son, not three Sons; one Holy Spirit, not three Holy Spirits.

And in this Trinity none is before or after another; none is greater or less than another;

but the whole three persons are coeternal with each other and coequal so that in all things, as has been stated above, the Trinity in Unity and Unity in Trinity is to be worshiped.

Therefore, whoever desires to be saved must think thus about the Trinity.

But it is also necessary for everlasting salvation that one faithfully believe the incarnation of our Lord Jesus Christ.

Therefore, it is the right faith that we believe and confess that our Lord Jesus Christ, the Son of God, is at the same time both God and man.

He is God, begotten from the substance of the Father before all ages; and He is man, born from the substance of His mother in this age:

perfect God and perfect man, composed of a rational soul and human flesh;

equal to the Father with respect to His divinity, less than the Father with respect to His humanity.

Although He is God and man, He is not two, but one Christ:

one, however, not by the conversion of the divinity into flesh but by the assumption of the humanity into God;

one altogether, not by confusion of substance, but by unity of person.

For as the rational soul and flesh is one man, so God and man is one Christ,

who suffered for our salvation, descended into hell, rose again on the third day from the dead,

ascended into heaven, and is seated at the right hand of the Father, from whence He will come to judge the living and the dead.

At His coming all people will rise again with their bodies and give an account con-concerning their own deeds.

And those who have done good will enter into eternal life, and those who have done evil into eternal fire.

This is the catholic faith; whoever does not believe it faithfully and firmly cannot be saved.

KEEPING THE HOLY TRINITY
IN BALANCE

*T*HROUGHOUT THE AGES, Christians readily accepted the Trinitarian theology, so painstakingly worked out by the early church fathers, and modern Christians embrace this definition of the faith. Yet today, as in ages past, the old deviations from the church universal continually re-emerge, in the form of Unitarianism, Universalism, ethical humanism, nature worship, polytheistic veneration of multiple deities, agnosticism, and countless other variations. As noted in Chapter Seven, the followers of these revisionist dogmas almost always adhere to the core ethical and moral teachings of our Lord and Savior, so that these believers should be respected, not despised, engaged in calm and rational debate, and above all, loved as fellow followers of the Word.

These diverse believers pose much less of a threat to the continued vitality of Christianity than those Trinitarians who venerate one or two heads of the Triune God but not all three. For this discussion it is useful to focus on the predominant or archetypical attributes of the three parts of God. God the Father is most clearly associated with *power, might,* and *majesty.* God the Son is most specifically defined by *love,* the core of the Gospel. And as Saint John clearly told us, God the Spirit encompasses the concept of *truth (John 14:16-17, 16:7-13).* More precisely, truth is defined by the constituent parts of the moral and ethical code, which Christ Himself in the Gospels commanded as every Christian's duty (as summarized from a superficial reading of Saint Matthew's Gospel): worship God, have faith, be a witness to your faith but do not seek recognition for your good deeds and undergo persecution if necessary. Feed the hungry, give drink to those who thirst, clothe the naked, give and lend to those in need, try to heal the sick, minister to the blind and the deaf and the lame, try to help the mentally ill to recover (drive out evil spirits), provide for the little children, be kind to strangers and be kind to prisoners. Love your enemies, be a peacemaker, forgive, do not be angry or vengeful, do not condemn or judge others, show mercy, reconcile with and satisfy your accusers. Do not murder, steal, lie, slander, envy, commit adultery, be lustful or engage in sexual immorality. Honor your father and mother. Do not accumulate wealth, or be self-indulgent or greedy, and do not be obsessive about material needs. Be meek, humble; be a servant and not a master.*

Psalm 145 captures these three divine essences of power, love, and truth:
> I will extol you, my God and King,
>> and bless your name forever and ever. . . .
>>> [Power]
> Great is the Lord, and greatly to be praised,
>> and his greatness is unsearchable.
> One generation shall commend your
>> works to another,
>>> and shall declare your mighty acts.
> On the glorious splendor of your majesty,
>> and on your wondrous works,
>>> I will meditate. . . .
>>>> [Love]
> The Lord is gracious and merciful,
>> slow to anger and abounding in
>>> steadfast love.
> The Lord is good to all,
>> and his mercy is over all that he has
>>> made. . . .
>>>> [Truth]
> The Lord is faithful in all his words
>> and kind in all his works. . . .
> The Lord is righteous in all his ways
>> and kind in all his works.
> The Lord is near to all who call on him,
>> to all who call on him in truth. . . .

A preoccupation with godly power, but without interweaving truth and love, leads to intolerance, condemnation, and elitism. In the past it led directly to the Inquisition and burning at the stake.

A single-minded embrace of God's love, without regard to divine power and truth, starts the Christian down the very slippery slope of situation ethics and moral relativism.

A fixation on truth unalloyed by love and God's power (as distinguished from mere human power) causes the Christian to have too high an opinion of his own wisdom, to discard the great virtue of humility, and to trust in human deeds and words rather than in God's Holy creation and His Holy Scripture. (It should be apparent that we are touching here on one of the great weaknesses of the Protestant Reformation, especially its Calvinist branch).

If we Christians can only cling to the Triune God, God the Father, God the Son, and God the Holy Spirit, we will go from strength to strength, and virtue to virtue, and with goodness, love, and mercy until the very last day.

* The connectivity of God's moral and ethical code to truth as attributed to the Holy Spirit is made manifest in *Ezekial 36:27:* "And I will put my Spirit within you, and cause you to walk in my statutes and be careful to obey my rules."

Chapter Eleven
Your Own THOUGHTS

*I*F YOU WANT TO PUBLISH YOUR VIEWS, exchange them with others, or learn of other peoples' opinions, see our website at www.practicalchristianguide.com.

How do you explain Cain's killing of Abel?

_____

_____

_____

_____

What significance does Cain's killing of Abel have for Christianity?

_____

_____

_____

_____

Do you think that I am going too far in suggesting that God's plan for humans on earth included the development of democratic government?

_____

_____

_____

_____

How do you support or oppose the idea that God's plan led to democracy?

_____

_____

_____

_____

Do you believe in Biblical inerrancy?

_____

_____

_____

_____

What is the basis for your belief?

_____

_____

_____

_____

_____

_____

_____

_____

_____

_____

If you do not believe in Biblical inerrancy, what parts of the Bible do you think are true and what parts of the Bible do you think are false? State the bases for your answer.

_____

_____

_____

_____

_____

_____

_____

Do you think that God is bound by the laws of nature? Explain your answer.

_____

_____

_____

_____

_____

_____

_____

_____

_____

_____

Do you believe miracles ever happen? Do you believe miracles stopped happening at some point? If so, when? And why was this?

_____

_____

_____

_____

Do you believe that miracles happen nowadays?

_____

_____

_____

_____

Explain the basis for your belief or disbelief in miracles.

_____

_____

_____

_____

_____

_____

_____

_____

_____

_____

If you disbelieve in miracles that occurred later than the restoration of sight to Saint Paul in the book of Acts, how do you explain all the testimony regarding miracles preserved in the annals of the Catholic Church?

_____

_____

_____

_____

_____

Do you have a rational explanation for the miracle of Noah's ark? If so, what is it?

_____

_____

_____

_____

_____

Have you ever witnessed one or more miracles? Please describe it or them.

_____

_____

_____

_____

_____

Do you know of a miracle or miracles (other than those reported in the Bible and those authenticated by the Catholic Church) in which you were not personally involved, that is or are so well established that you believe it or they occurred? Please describe it or them.

_____

_____

_____

_____

_____

_____

_____

_____

What do you think about my suggestion that human beings were already in existence when Adam and Eve were created?

_____

_____

_____

_____

_____

_____

_____

_____

_____

If you disagree with my suggestion about Adam and Eve not being the first human beings, what is your explanation for their children taking spouses?

_____

_____

_____

_____

_____

_____

Do you believe the prophecies of Christ's birth, ministry, and crucifixion came to pass?

_____

_____

_____

_____

_____

_____

Can you point to other Biblical prophecies (book, chapter, and verse, please) that were fulfilled?

_____

_____

_____

_____

_____

Can you point to other Biblical prophecies (book, chapter, and verse, please) that have not been fulfilled?

_____

_____

_____

_____

_____

_____

_____

Which of these unfulfilled prophecies yet may be fulfilled as part of God's plan?

_____

_____

_____

_____

_____

_____

_____

_____

_____

_____

_____

For which of these unfulfilled Biblical prophecies do you believe is too late to be fulfilled or otherwise will not work out?

_____

_____

_____

_____

_____

_____

_____

_____

_____

_____

With what degree of confidence can religious leaders set a date on which a prophecy will be fulfilled? Why?

_____

_____

_____

_____

_____

_____

_____

Do you think there have ever been any true relics preserved by the church?

_____

_____

_____

_____

_____

Do you think there still remain true relics preserved by the church? Explain.

_____

_____

_____

_____

Do you think the Shroud of Turin is a true relic? Explain.

_____

_____

_____

_____

_____

_____

Do you disagree with my statement that no events of the Bible have been shown by geological or archaeological evidence not to have occurred? If so, state your proof about that.

_____

_____

_____

_____

_____

_____

_____

_____

Do you agree that both the universal church and the Protestant denominations became pharisaic about innovative thinking?

_____

_____

_____

_____

_____

_____

_____

What do you think about Capernican-Galilean astronomy? Explain.

_____

_____

_____

_____

_____

_____

_____

Do you believe in heaven? If so, where is it and what is it like? What is your basis, Biblical and otherwise, for your belief about heaven?

_____

_____

_____

_____

_____

_____

_____

_____

_____

_____

_____

Has Christianity been strengthened by the individualism that is connected with the Great Awakenings? Or has it been weakened? Or has it been strengthened in some ways and weakened in others? Explain.

_____

_____

_____

_____

_____

_____

_____

Can Darwinian theory and Christianity be reconciled? If so, how?

_____

_____

_____

_____

_____

_____

_____

_____

_____

_____

_____

Does the granting of a prayer that asks God to depart from the natural order amount to a miracle? If not, why not?

_____

_____

_____

_____

_____

Are such prayers ever granted?

_____

_____

_____

Do you believe that prayer is helpful to the one who prays? How?

_____

_____

_____

_____

_____

_____

_____

_____

Do you believe that prayer is helpful to the one for whom you pray — if that person knows of the prayer? Or if that person does not know of the prayer? Explain.

_____

_____

_____

_____

_____

_____

_____

_____

Can Christianity and Freudian psychology be reconciled? Why or why not?

_____

_____

_____

_____

_____

_____

_____

_____

_____

Can communism or socialism, as long as it does not involve dictatorship or other repression of personal rights, be reconciled with Christianity? Why or why not?

_____

_____

_____

_____

_____

_____

_____

_____

Has God ever changed? If so, when and how? Have human perceptions of God changed? When and how?

_____

_____

_____

_____

_____

_____

_____

_____

Is the physical temple going to be restored in Jerusalem? If so, when? What is your Biblical basis for believing that the temple will be rebuilt?

_____

_____

_____

_____

_____

_____

_____

_____

_____

How do you deal with scriptures such as *Matthew 24:29-31, Mark 9:1* and *13:3-27,* and *Luke 21:27-28* concerning the expectation that Christ soon would return to earth?

_____

_____

_____

_____

_____

_____

_____

_____

Is there any relevance in the human activities of farming, gardening, and fishing, in connection with the miracle of Christ feeding the multitudes? Explain.

_____

_____

_____

_____

_____

_____

_____

_____

Are there any aspects of human activities of providing health care that have a connection with the miracles of Christ's healing? Explain.

_____

_____

_____

_____

_____

_____

_____

_____

_____

What is your belief about the Rapture? When will it occur? What is the scriptural basis for your belief?

_____

_____

_____

_____

_____

_____

_____

_____

What is your explanation for the passage in _Mark 12:17:_ "Render to Caesar the things that are Caesar's and to God the things that are God's?"

_____

_____

_____

_____

_____

_____

_____

_____

_____

What are your opinions about theocracies, both autocratic and democratic?

_____

_____

_____

_____

_____

_____

_____

_____

_____

To what extent should secularization be encouraged in Christian nations and why?

_____

_____

_____

_____

_____

_____

_____

_____

_____

_____

To what extent should secularization be encouraged in Muslim nations and why?

_____

_____

_____

_____

_____

_____

_____

_____

Have you ever gone to any of your Jewish, Muslim, Unitarian, or agnostic friends and told them that their immortal souls are in danger because they have not converted to Christianity? If not, why not?

_____

_____

_____

_____

_____

_____

_____

_____

What does the Word mean in the First Chapter of the Gospel of Saint John?

_____

_____

_____

_____

_____

_____

_____

_____

Please point to any verse in the Gospels that tells us that we must worship the person of Jesus.

_____

_____

_____

If Jesus is the vine, God is the vine dresser, and the faithful Christians are the fruiting branches, what or who are the grapes? Explain.

_____

_____

_____

_____

_____

State what you believe to be the list of Christian ethical and moral values.

_____

_____

_____

_____

_____

_____

_____

_____

_____

What happens when a society tries to drive out or eradicate the Christian faith?

_____

_____

_____

_____

_____

_____

_____

_____

_____

_____

How did Christianity, then wholly contained within the Roman Empire, survive not one, but seven great persecutions when the authorities tried to wipe out the faith?

_____

_____

_____

_____

_____

_____

_____

What percentage of the people of a nation must be practicing Christians in order for the faith to survive and flourish?

_____

_____

_____

In what countries other than the United States would you be content to live and why?

_____

_____

_____

Do non-Christians have better morals and ethics if they live in a Christian society? Why is this so, or not so?

_____

_____

_____

_____

Of what significance is it that Saint John in his Gospel mentions Jesus washing His Disciples' feet at their last gathering, but omits the account of the Last Supper?

_____

_____

_____

_____

What is the meaning of Jesus' reference to Himself so often as the Son of Man?

_____

_____

_____

_____

_____

_____

_____

_____

Why did Christianity not become a minor sect of Judaism? Why did Christianity not become part of the polytheistic Greco-Roman pantheon? Why did Christianity not get taken over by Arianism (a sort of Unitarianism), Gnosticism (a sort of universalism), or the Manichean faith (which included a large component of nature worship)?

_____

_____

_____

_____

_____

_____

_____

_____

_____

_____

_____

What is your definition of the Holy Spirit?

_____

_____

_____

How could the Blessed Virgin have known of the central beliefs of Christianity even before Jesus was born?

_____

_____

_____

_____

_____

Why did the male Disciples, except for Saint John, desert Jesus as he headed for the Crucifixion, whereas the Blessed Virgin, Saint Mary Magdalene, the other Saint Mary, and Saint Martha all stayed by His side?

_____

_____

_____

_____

_____

_____

_____

_____

_____

_____

_____

Why was the Blessed Virgin so trashed in the Reformation?

_____

_____

_____

_____

_____

_____

_____

Why does the Blessed Virgin occupy a relatively minor status in the Protestant denominations?

_____

_____

_____

_____

_____

_____

_____

_____

_____

_____

In what ways were the lives and status of women improved by the coming of Christianity?

_____

_____

_____

_____

_____

_____

_____

In light of the protection that Christianity brought to women, do we need to be concerned about the prevalence of divorce and unwed motherhood in modern Christian society? Why or why not?

_____

_____

_____

_____

_____

_____

_____

_____

_____

Discuss chivalry in the context of Christianity.

_____

_____

_____

_____

_____

_____

_____

_____

How do you explain the events of the life of Saint Joan of Arc?

_____

_____

_____

_____

_____

_____

_____

_____

_____

_____

Was there any justification whatever for the destruction in the Reformation of paintings, statuary, metal castings, carvings, stained glass windows, murals, frescos, inlaid and embossed flooring, illuminated manuscripts, vestments, silver communion services, and relics? If so, explain fully.

_____

_____

_____

_____

_____

_____

Of what significance were the lengthy oral sermons that were a principal feature of Protestant worship?

_____

_____

_____

_____

_____

_____

_____

_____

_____

_____

_____

Can the Reformation be viewed as the increased domination of men over women? Explain.

_____

_____

_____

_____

_____

Was there any justification for the killing of Anne Boleyn? Explain.

_____

_____

_____

_____

_____

_____

Was there any justification for the killing of the "witches" of Salem, Massachusetts? Explain.

_____

_____

_____

_____

_____

In what ways did the martyrdom of Saint James the Younger parallel that of Jesus?

_____

_____

_____

_____

_____

_____

Is Christianity best defended or upheld based on reason or based on faith? What is the basis for your conclusion?

_____

_____

_____

_____

_____

_____

Do you agree with the pre-Reformation Catholic Church, Martin Luther, or Saint James the Younger concerning works versus faith?

_____

_____

_____

_____

_____

Is it right to seek justification from both faith and good works? Explain.

_____

_____

_____

_____

_____

Does the voluntary doing of good works tend to enhance faith?

_____

_____

_____

_____

_____

Does the strength of your faith tend to motivate you to do good works?

_____

_____

_____

_____

_____

_____

Can the doing of genuine Christian good works (not just things to aggrandize the church or its leaders) have any negative impact on faith?

_____

_____

_____

_____

_____

_____

_____

_____

_____

Can the building up of faith ever have any negative impact on doing good works?

_____

_____

_____

_____

_____

_____

_____

_____

_____

What is your religion, and how did you get to where you are in your present faith?

_____

_____

_____

_____

_____

_____

_____

_____

_____

Have you ever had a religious experience? If so, please describe it.

_____

_____

_____

_____

_____

_____

_____

_____

_____

_____

Do you believe that religious art tends to enhance religious beliefs? Why or why not?

_____

_____

_____

_____

_____

_____

_____

_____

_____

What do you think about the Council of Nicea? Do you believe that the Holy Spirit guided those who participated in the council?

_____

_____

_____

_____

_____

_____

_____

_____

_____

What do you think happened to the water and blood that came out of Jesus' side at the Crucifixion when the spear was thrust into Him?

_____

_____

_____

_____

_____

Do you think it is unreasonable for the blood and the water, or either of them, to have entered botanical genetic material and have been preserved to the present time? Why?

_____

_____

_____

_____

How can Catholic and Protestant positions on the Eucharist be reconciled, or do you believe they cannot be?

_____

_____

_____

_____

_____

How does the human function of grafting scions into root stock fit into the viniculture analogy in *Saint John's Gospel, 15:1-7*, or does it not?

_____

_____

_____

_____

_____

Are there pathways by which the natural order of botanic growth and reproduction tend to support and make more meaningful certain Christian beliefs? Describe some of these. Can an understanding of these functions lead to a better connection of environmentalism to Christianity?

_____

_____

_____

_____

_____

Do you believe Saint Paul's epistles to be inerrant? If so, how do you deal with his pronouncement about seeing through a glass darkly in *1 Corinthians 13:12?* If not, how can we avoid a path of deconstruction and debunking the Pauline epistles?

_____

_____

_____

_____

_____

What should be the role of women in the church? What is the basis for your opinion? What scriptural support do you have for your opinion?

_____

_____

_____

_____

_____

What should be the role of husband and wife in the marital union? What scriptural support do you have for your opinion?

_____

_____

_____

_____

_____

Is it possible that we and our fellow Christians are brothers and sisters in Christ, not only figuratively, but in actuality? Explain how this could or could not be so.

_____

_____

_____

_____

_____

Do you agree that there are Trinitarian precursors in the Old Testament, or do you regard the Biblical references in Chapter Ten to be more associated with some other meaning (or to be meaningless)? Please discuss.

_____

_____

_____

_____

_____

When do you believe that the divine Jesus Christ came into being? What is the basis for your opinion?

_____

_____

_____

_____

_____

When do you believe that the divine Holy Spirit came into being? What is the basis for your opinion?

_____

_____

_____

_____

_____

_____

Some examples of what are deemed proto-Trinitarian references in the Bible are given in Chapter Ten. Are you able to add others?

_____

_____

_____

_____

_____

What is your reaction to the suggestion in Chapter Ten that the Fall might have been precipitated in part by Eve's taking from, adding to, and altering God's Word?

_____

_____

_____

_____

_____

What is your explanation of the Transfiguration?

_____

_____

_____

_____

_____

What was the role of Saint James the Elder as recorded by Scripture?

_____

_____

_____

_____

_____

Could Saint James the Elder have reappeared and performed miracles post-Scripturally and after his death, as asserted in Chapter Ten? Why or why not?

_____

_____

_____

_____

_____

How do you explain Christ's remaining at the Transfiguration after Moses and Elijah disappeared?

_____

_____

_____

_____

_____

Can you make a case for the worship and glorification of Jesus Christ and the Holy Spirit based on the Gospels alone. Explain.

_____

_____

_____

_____

_____

_____

Are the terms "the world, the flesh, and the devil" used in the baptismal creed merely archaic and poetic, or do they have current meaning? Explain.

_____

_____

_____

_____

_____

_____

How and why did the Holy Trinity strengthen the church in its early formative years?

_____

_____

_____

_____

_____

Of what value and significance is the use of the number three?

_____

_____

_____

_____

_____

_____

What is your reaction to the Athanasian Creed? Explain.

_____

_____

_____

_____

_____

_____

Do you agree with the three prime attributes of God the Father, God the Son, and God the Holy Spirit as power, love, and truth, respectively, as suggested in Chapter Ten? If not, what attributes do you believe are the most important to each part of the Trinity and why?

_____

_____

_____

_____

What can be the consequences to the church of the concentration on God's power to the exclusion of God's love and truth? Explain.

_____

_____

_____

_____

_____

What can be the consequences to the church of a concentration on God's love to the exclusion of God's power and truth?

_____

_____

_____

_____

_____

What can be the consequences to the church of a concentration on God's truth to the exclusion of God's power and love?

_____

_____

_____

_____

_____

What is the connection between the Tower of Babel event and the Pentecost event?

_____

_____

_____

_____

Have any of the aspects of the Tower of Babel event played out in modern times? Explain.

_____

_____

_____

_____

Have any of the aspects of the Pentecost event played out in modern times? Explain.

_____

_____

_____

_____

_____

_____

_____

With what statements or suggestions in the book do you disagree and why?

_____

_____

_____

_____

_____

_____

_____

_____

_____

Have you benefitted in any way from this book? If so, in what way?

_____

_____

_____

_____

_____

_____

_____

_____

_____

_____

Has your faith been undermined or attacked in any way by this book? If so, how?

_____

_____

_____

_____

_____

_____

_____

_____

_____

Are there things the book should have said that were omitted? If so, what?

_____

_____

_____

_____

_____

_____

_____

_____

_____

_____

EPILOGUE

EVEN DURING MY MOST DOCTRINAIRE UNITARIAN DAYS, I believed that God had at least three essential functions, first, the Creation, of course; second, guiding and directing evolution; and third, tamping down both natural and human developments when they seemingly got out of hand. The last function in my conception was not unlike the nemesis invariably visited upon humankind when too infected with hubris, so familiar in Greek mythology.

This brings us to the Tower of Babel account, *Genesis 11:1-9:*

Now the whole earth had one language and the same words. And as people migrated from the east, they found a plain in the land of Shinar and settled there. And they said to one another, "Come, let us make bricks, and burn them thoroughly." And they had brick for stone, and bitumen for mortar. Then they said, "Come, let us build ourselves a city and a tower with its top in the heavens, and let us make a name for ourselves, lest we be dispersed over the face of the whole earth." And the LORD came down to see the city and the tower, which the children of man had built. And the LORD said, "Behold, they are one people, and they have all one language, and this is only the beginning of what they will do. And nothing that they propose to do will now be impossible for them. Come, let us go down and there confuse their language, so that they may not understand one another's speech." So the LORD dispersed them from there over the face of all the earth, and they left off building the city. Therefore its name was called Babel, because there the LORD confused the language of all the earth. And from there the LORD dispersed them over the face of all the earth.

HUMANS HAD BECOME PRIDEFUL AND ARROGANT. They undertook to build an incredibly tall building that would thrust up into the heavens. Notice the blatant materialism of this foolish undertaking. Not surprisingly, God decided to stop this folly, and He did. Not only was the structure brought to an end, but also great mines, workshops, and urban organization were dismantled. The workers were scattered all over the earth, and they no longer communicated in the same language, for God had given them numerous different languages instead.

This is an example of an Old Testament story that, in addition to its literal truth, has resounded and reverberated throughout the ages.

In recent times the erection of the world's tallest buildings has been followed often by hard times in which not only those who constructed the building but also many other workers have lost their jobs, have lost their homes, and have been driven away to other places. The building of the Empire State Building ushered in the Great Depression of 1929; the erection of the Sears Tower was followed by the recession of 1974; the dot.com bubble burst in 2000, shortly after completion of the Twin Towers in Kuala Lampur; and before the Burj Khalifa (Dubai Tower) could be completed in that year, the Great Recession of 2008 struck. Sadly, the nemesis for the World Trade Center came not in the form of mere recession and economic hardship, but by physical destruction accompanied by horrendous loss of human life. The new World Trade Center building is planned to be the tallest building in the United States. You may wish to make appropriate adjustments to your 401(k) account shortly before it is completed in 2013.

The New Testament analogue to the multi-lingual diaspora following Babel's collapse is the account of the Pentecost in *Acts 2:1-12*:

> When the day of Pentecost arrived, they were all together in one place. And suddenly there came from heaven a sound like a mighty rushing wind, and it filled the entire house where they were sitting. And divided tongues as of fire appeared to them and rested on each one of them. And they were all filled with the Holy Spirit and began to speak in other tongues as the Spirit gave them utterance.

Now there were dwelling in Jerusalem Jews, devout men from every nation under heaven. And at this sound the multitude came together, and they were bewildered, because each one was hearing them speak in his own language. And they were amazed and astonished, saying, "Are not all these who are speaking Galileans? And how is it that we hear, each of us in his own native language? Parthians and Medes and Elamites and residents of Mesopotamia, Judea and Cappadocia, Pontus and Asia, Phrygia and

Pamphylia, Egypt and the parts of Libya belonging to Cyrene, and visitors from Rome, both Jews and proselytes, Cretans and Arabians – we hear them telling in our own tongues the mighty works of God." And all were amazed and perplexed, saying to one another, "What does this mean?"

After being given the gift of speaking in all the tongues known in that part of the world, the faithful Christians in fulfillment of the commission by Jesus, *Mark 16:15*, began to "Go into all the world and proclaim the gospel to the whole creation." Ever since Christian missionaries have braved every hardship, have fearlessly faced every adversity, and have been martyred by the thousands in the unending work of proclaiming the Gospel to the world.

Carrying forward the ancient tradition of communicating in the languages of others, Christian missionaries have ordinarily been the first to reduce primitive languages to writing and to provide Biblical translations in these native tongues. Whereas the Babelians departed in hopelessness and with an inability to communicate with their brethren, the Pentecostals went into the world boldly and filled with the Holy Spirit, speaking not only in their native tongues, but also in newly-learned languages. The great work of the Christian missionaries has gone forward unabated. It has been humble, not prideful and arrogant. It has not been met with nemesis, but only with the everlasting gratitude of the Almighty.

Surely God is equally pleased with those, to pursue the dichotomy noted in Chapter Seven, with those who do not work directly to propagate the worship of Christ's person, but who labor instead to extend the Word, the ethical and moral grapes of God's vineyard. These laborers include Peace Corps volunteers, the noble Médecins Sans Frontières, removers of land mines and cluster bombs, USAID and UNICEF employees, international human rights advocates, and humanitarian aid workers of every kind and description.

Where would you prefer to stand: with the builders of Babel or with the Pentecostal missionaries? Remember that the accumulation of wealth and power that is emblematic of building vast towers is not destined to provide rewards in this world or the next. "Look at the birds of the air: they neither sow nor reap nor gather into barns, and yet your heavenly Father feeds them. Are you not of more value than they? And which of you by being anxious can add a single hour to his span of life? And why are you anxious about clothing?

Consider the lilies of the field, how they grow: they neither toil nor spin, yet I tell you, even Solomon in all his glory was not arrayed like one of these. But if God so clothes the grass of the field, which today is alive and tomorrow is thrown into the oven, will he not much more clothe you, O you of little faith? Therefore do not be anxious, saying, 'What shall we eat?' or 'What shall we drink?' or 'What shall we wear?' For the Gentiles seek after all these things, and your heavenly Father knows that you need them all. But seek first the kingdom of God and his righteousness, and all these things will be added to you" *(Matthew 6:26-33).*

$\mathcal{A}$PPENDIX

$\mathcal{T}$HE APPENDIX OFFERS SIXTY-THREE MEDIEVAL, RENAISSANCE, BAROQUE, AND MANNERIST paintings formed into a perpetual weekly calendar, five for each month save February which has four, and four for the holy days of Palm Sunday, Good Friday, Easter, and Ascension of Our Lord, which are governed by the lunar calendar and shift from year to year. Most of the weeks are marked by festivals of Christianity such as the Annunciation, the Nativity, the Circumcision, Epiphany, and the Presentation at the Temple, or by pre-Reformation saints' days. I have added appropriate religious paintings that fit the modern holidays of Mother's Day, Father's Day, and Thanksgiving, and, of course, a portrait of Martin Luther by Cranach the Elder *(figure 10-4)* to mark Reformation Sunday (Cranach was the best man at Luther's wedding.). I could not resist including Fra Angelico's *Annunciation (figure 3-4)* and Rogier Van Der Weyden's *Descent from the Cross (figure M-2),* which, as recorded in the Introduction, played such a vital role in my own conversion to Christianity.

Those who are interested in Judeo-Christian numerology may wish to ponder the above number sixty-three. It is a trinitarian multiple, the product of three numbers, consisting of the Holy Trinity squared and the number seven. Seven has exceptionally rich numerological significance: seven days of creation *(Genesis 2:2),* seven days' march (seven times on the seventh day) around Jericho with seven rams' horns and seven priests *(Joshua 6:3-5),* seven wounds of Christ at the Crucifixion (flagellation, crown of thorns, hands and feet pierced by nails, spear thrust to the side; *Matthew 27:26, 29, 35;* and *John 19:34),* and numerous references in Revelation including seven churches *(1:4),* seven spirits before the throne *(1:4),* seven seals *(8:1),* seven trumpets *(8:6),* seven angels *(8:6),* seven plagues *(15:1),* and seven bowls *(16:1).*

These magnificent works of art are in the public domain on account of their antiquity, so reproduction of them is freely allowed. They would make attractive church bulletin covers, computer screen savers, or note cards. Feel free to obtain your set of these paintings by visiting our website at www.practicalchristianguide.com.

It often has been said that a picture is worth a thousand words. Goodness knows how many thousands or tens of thousands of words are equaled by the great masterpieces of religious art. The principal Calvinist church in our city had two very notable pastors over a span of nearly the second half of the twentieth century. Church services at which they preached were packed with worshipers. Their extremely fine sermons were broadcast on the radio, reproduced in the press, and distributed in printed form. Yet now, after a few years have gone by, few people, if any, can remember a word of what was preached by them. On the other hand, if you have ever seen, even a copy, of Rembrandt's *Return of the Prodigal* or Bellini's *Baptism of Christ,* you could never put the image out of your mind.

The value of religious art as a part of Christian worship was well recognized by the early church. Consider the following excerpts from the proceedings of the Seventh Council of Nicea in 787 AD:

Icons remind us of Christ's life among men.

That which the narrative declares in writing is the same as that which the icon does in colors ...

[A]s when we receive the sound of reading with our ears, we transmit it to our mind, so by looking with our eyes at the painted icons, we are enlightened in our mind. Through two things following each other, that is by reading and also seeing the reproduction of the painting, we learn the same thing, that is, how to recall what has taken place. The operation of these two most basic senses is also found conjoined in the Song of Songs, where it says, "Show me thy face, and cause me to hear thy voice; for thy voice is sweet, and thy countenance is beautiful."

The representation of scenes in colours follows the narrative of the gospel, and the narrative of the gospel follows the narrative of the paintings.... When we see on an icon the angel bringing the good news to the Virgin, we must certainly bring to mind that the angel Gabriel was sent from God to the virgin. And he came to her and said: "Hail, O favored one, the Lord is with you. Blessed are you among women" *(Luke 1:26-28).* Thus from the gospel we have heard of the mystery communicated to the Virgin through the angel, and this way we are reminded of it. Now when we see the same thing on an icon we perceive the event with great emphasis.

For reasons that are difficult to comprehend, the aroused public in the Protestant Reformation (except in Lutheran domains where they were restrained by the civil authorities at Luther's request) engaged in furious spasms of iconoclasm, in the course of which were destroyed tens of thousands of Christian paintings,

Franz Hegenberg (Dutch, c. 1540-1590).
Iconoclasm in a Flemish Church, 1588.
Woodcut.
BRITISH MUSEUM, LONDON.

carvings, metal castings, statuary, tapestries, wall decorations, ceiling decorations, floor decorations, stained glass, illuminated manuscripts, robes and vestments, communion services, relics and reliquaries, and other adornments of the church. They were slashed, smashed, and burned by sword, hammer, and fire. Still other thousands of these precious objects were destroyed by Muslims in the seventh through the sixteenth centuries, French Revolutionaries in the late eighteenth century, communists in the twentieth century, and the artillery fire and bombings from countless wars and uprisings down to the end of the twentieth century. I am amazed that the remaining heritage of Christian art is as rich and varied as it is. The part of this treasure that remains with us deserves to be brought back into our religious services and private devotions. By this means our faith will be enlivened and enriched.

I express my profound thanks to Henry Hilston, undergraduate art history student of the University of North Carolina at Greensboro, for locating, describing, and reproducing the sixty-three masterpieces of religious art contained in this appendix.

$\mathcal{J}$ANUARY

1st Sunday (1-1)

Circumcision of Christ *(January 3rd)*
LUKE 2.21

Tintoretto, *Circumcision of Christ,* 1587
ITALIAN MANNERISM

Located at the Scuola Grande di San Rocco

$\mathcal{F}$OLLOWING THE JEWISH TRADITION forged between God and Abraham, Christ was taken to the Temple eight days after his birth to be circumcised. Christ's circumcision can be understood as the first time Christ shed blood for humanity, and so it is the beginning of the redemption of mankind through Christ.

JANUARY

2nd Sunday (1-2)

Epiphany *(January 6th)*
MATTHEW 2.1-12

Peter Paul Rubens, *Adoration of the Magi,* 1628-1629
FLEMISH BAROQUE

Located at the Museo Nacional del Prado, Madrid

*H*AVING SEEN THE STAR IN THE SKY, three gentile magi from the east came and visited Christ so that they might pay their respects to the King of the Jews. In Western Christianity, the Epiphany marks the moment when the world recognized Christ's divinity.

*J*ANUARY

3rd Sunday (1-3)

Baptism of Christ *(January 9th)*
MARK 1.9-11, LUKE 3.21-22, MATTHEW 3.13-17

Giovanni Bellini, *Baptism of Christ,* 1500-1502
ITALIAN VENETIAN RENAISSANCE

Located at the Santa Corona, Vicenza

*J*OHN THE BAPTIST INITIATED THE RITE of Baptism as an act of repentance in anticipation of the coming of Christ; the rite symbolically washes the sins of humankind away. When Christ participated in the rite, the Spirit of God came down from heaven and marked him as the Son of God.

NOTE: *Although art historians are not necessarily in agreement, the author believes the three women are the Blessed Virgin (closest to Christ) and His two halfsisters based on the text* Matthew 13:55. *Just as Dan Brown in* The Da Vinci Code *claimed that there was a code embedded in* The Mona Lisa, *it may be suggested that a code is embedded in these three female figures in* Baptism of Christ, *to be decoded by the information set out in the text on pages 61–64.*

$\mathcal{J}$ANUARY

4th Sunday (1-4)

Conversion of St. Paul *(January 25th)*
ACTS 9.1-19

Caravaggio, *Conversion of St. Paul,* 1600
ITALIAN BAROQUE

Located at the Odescalchi Balbi Collection, Rome

"Saul, Saul, why do you persecute me?" *(Acts 9.4).*

SAUL was a zealous persecutor of the Christians. But in Saul God saw the possibility of someone who could spread the message of Christ's redemption to the Gentiles. As Paul he became an outspoken advocate of Christianity and engaged in missionary work throughout the Roman Empire.

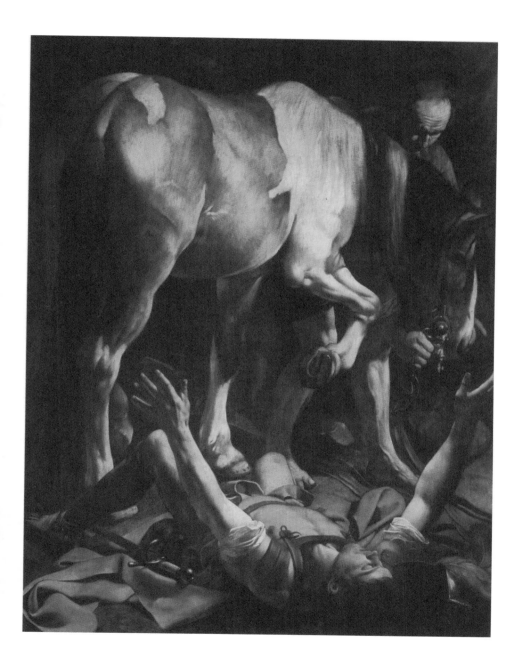

JANUARY

5th Sunday (1-5)

St. John Chrysostom (The Golden Mouth) *(January 27th)*
B. 347 D. 407

Sebastiano Del Piombo, *St. John Chrysostom,* 1510-1511
ITALIAN VENETIAN RENAISSANCE

Located at San Giovanni Crisostomo, Venice

JOHN CHRYSOSTOM WAS AN OUTSPOKEN LEADER of the early Church who delivered sermons against impropriety in the Church. He was especially interested in reforming those who headed the Church. He served as the Archbishop of Constantinople from 397 until 407 and penned many theological works, including a new liturgy for the Church.

*F*EBRUARY

1st Sunday (2-1)

Presentation of Christ in the Temple *(February 2nd)*
LUKE 2.22-38

Hans Memling, *Presentation of Christ,* 1463
NORTHERN TRADITION

Museo Nacional del Prado, Madrid

*T*HE PRESENTATION IN THE TEMPLE, like the circumcision which precedes it in the scripture, shows that Jesus Christ was fulfilling the Law as laid down in the Old Testament. It is also when Simeon the Righteous gives a prophecy about Christ, which says he will be "a light for revelation to the Gentiles and for Glory to your people Israel" *(Luke 2.29-33).*

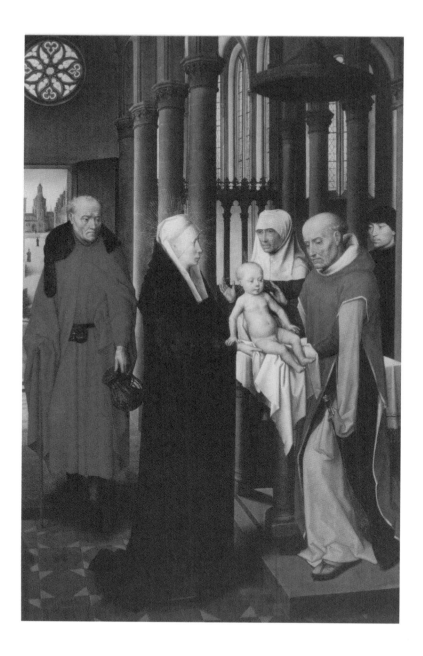

$\mathcal{F}$EBRUARY

2nd Sunday (2-2)

Transfiguration *(February 13th)*
MARK 9.2-13; LUKE 9.28-36; MATTHEW 17.1-13

Giovanni Bellini, *Transfiguration*, 1518-1520
ITALIAN FLORENTINE RENAISSANCE

Located at the Museo di Capodimonte, Naples

O N A HIGH SPOT (sometimes considered Mt. Tabor), Elijah (a prophet) and Moses (the bringer of the Law) appeared to Jesus; "And he was transfigured before them [the apostles], and his clothes became dazzling white, such as no one on earth could bleach them" *(Mark 9.2-3)*. Christ also confirms that Elijah has returned to earth (as John the Baptist) as it was prophesized *(Mark 9.11-14)*.

$\mathcal{F}$EBRUARY

3rd Sunday (2-3)

St. Matthias, Apostle *(February 24th)*
ACTS 1.15-26

Masolino da Panicale, *St. Matthias and Gregory the Great,*
1428-1429
EARLY ITALIAN RENAISSANCE

Located at the National Gallery, London

$\mathcal{M}$ATTHIAS WAS CHOSEN BY THE APOSTLES to replace Judas. Rarely depicted in art, he holds the means of his martyrdom (an axe) and is a balding man. According to the Golden Legend of Jacobus de Voragine, Matthias was a missionary, preacher, and performer of miracles.

$\mathcal{F}$EBRUARY

4th Sunday (2-4)

Elijah in the Wilderness
KINGS 19.1-18

Tintoretto, *Elijah Fed by an Angel,* 1577-1578
VENETIAN MANNERISM

Located at Scuola Grande di San Rocco, Venice

$\mathcal{E}$LIJAH DEFENDED JUDAISM AGAINST the false prophets of Baal and even killed the false prophets of Baal who were threatening his faith. After this deed, he went into the wilderness to die: "It is enough; now, O Lord, take away my life, for I am no better than my ancestors" *(1 Kings 19.4-5)*. But at the point of death, God provides sustenance for him, and he continues to live so that he might continue the fight against heresy.

$\mathcal{M}$ARCH

1st Sunday (3-1)

St. Thomas Aquinas, *(March 7th)*
B. 1225 D. 1274

Benozzo Gozzoli, *The Triumph of St. Thomas Aquinas,* 1471
ITALIAN, FLORENTINE RENAISSANCE

Located at the Musee de Louvre, Paris

*T*HOMAS AQUINAS WAS A GREAT THEOLOGIAN and philospher of the Middle Ages. A student of Albert the Great, Thomas studied Aristotle fastidiously — study which led to his attempts to reconcile faith and reason. He is perhaps best known for compiling the monolithic *Summa Theologiae,* an attempt to recount and comment upon Christian thought up to his time. This particular painting depicts his triumph over the Albigensian heretics. As a member of the Dominican order, it was his work to bring people to the true Faith.

$\mathcal{M}$ARCH

2nd Sunday (3-2)

Rebecca and Eliezer at the Well
GENESIS 24.1-50

Nicolas Poussin, *Rebecca at the Well,* 1648
FRENCH, CLASSICIST BAROQUE

Located at the Musee de Louvre, Paris

ABRAHAM, BEING OLD AND DESIRING A WIFE for his son Isaac, sent his servant to his people at Nahor. There, his servant made an entreaty to the God of his master that the chosen bride be marked, and so he found Rebecca by the well. Rebecca went on to marry Isaac, and when she was found to be barren, Isaac prayed to God that she be granted children *(Genesis 25.21-23).* The granting of a child to woman through divine will here mirrors the birth of Isaac from Sarah and also prefigures the Annunciation to Mary.

◌Ⲙarch

3rd Sunday (3-3)

St. Patrick, *(March 17th)*
B. 389 D. 444

The Lombard School, *St. Patrick Baptizing the Converts,*
15th century
Italian, International Style

Located at San Patrizio, Colzate

Ⲉ nslaved in his youth by the pagan Celts of Ireland, he eventually escaped as the result of a silent prayer to God. After study in France, he began to convert the pagans of the land and baptize them. Under his leadership the first See of Ireland was founded at Armagh. He is justly called the patron Saint of Ireland.

Ｍarch

4th Sunday (3-4)

The Annunciation, *(March 25th)*
Luke 1.26-38

Fra Angelico, *The Annunciation*, 1433-1434
Italian, Early Tuscan Renaissance

Located at the Convento di San Marco, Florence

And he [Gabriel] came to her and said, "Greetings, favored one! The Lord is with you ... And now, you will conceive in your womb and bear a son ..."

Gabriel came to Mary and announced that she would conceive a child through the grace of God, and thus begins the narrative of Christ's life according to Luke. Christ, conceived by God through the Holy Spirit, came to earth to redeem the sins of mankind.

ＭARCH

5th Sunday (3-5)

Moses Brings Water from the Rock
EXODUS 17.1-7

Tintoretto, *Moses Drawing Water from the Rock,* 1577
ITALIAN, VENETIAN MANNERISM

Located at the Scuola Grande di San Rocco, Venice

THE PEOPLE OF MOSES did not believe God was truly amongst them, and when they arrived at the wilderness of Sin there was no water to be found. Moses asked God to show Himself. God miraculously supplied water from a rock in the wilderness. Here God provides sustenance for His people even when they are unbelieving in Him.

*A*PRIL

1st Sunday (4-1)

St. Catherine of Siena, *(April 29th)*

Lucas Cranach the Elder, *The Mystic Marriage of St. Catherine,*
c. 1516
Northern Tradition

Located at the Szépmûvészeti Mûzeum, Budapest

CATHERINE OF SIENA was born the twenty-fifth child of a wool-dyer. Around the age of five, she experienced her first divine visions in which she witnessed the presence of the imperceptible in the earthly realm. She continued to have these visions for the remainder of her short life, and it is her visions for which she is known. In one of her visions, Catherine was mystically married to Jesus. This was not an unusual concept in medieval mysticism and was inspired by the *Song of Songs.* She also wrote theological works and attempted to mend the great schism between the papacies of Rome and Avignon.

$\mathcal{A}$PRIL

2nd Sunday (4-2)

God Responding to Job
JOB 38.1-42.6

William Blake, *The Lord Answering Job
from the Whirlwind,* 1803-1805
ENGLISH ROMANTICISM

*Located at the National Gallery of Scotland, Edinburgh
Presented by the Trustees of Mr. Graham Robertson 1949 through the Art Fund.*

GOD, FOLLOWING A CHALLENGE FROM SATAN, allowed Job's prosperous life to be destroyed by Satan *(Job 1-2).* Job's twist of fate led him to call himself a victim of injustice, and through a series of discourses with other men he developed this theme until in *Job 38* God appeared to him and refuted him. Ultimately Job retracted by saying, "Therefore I have uttered what I did not understand, things too wonderful for me, which I did not know" *(Job 42.3-4),* and he repented before God after having experienced God's power.

$\mathcal{A}$PRIL

3rd Sunday (4-3)

St. George, Martyr, *(April 23rd)*
ALIVE CIRCA 300 AD

Raphael, *St. George and the Dragon,* 1506
ITALIAN, FLORENTINE RENAISSANCE

Located at the National Gallery of Art, Washington, D.C.

ST. GEORGE IS BEST KNOWN FOR THE ACCOUNT contained in the Golden Legend by Jacobus de Voragine in which George is a Christian knight, a model of chivalry, who kills a venomous dragon thereby saving a young maiden from death. George lived in the Roman Empire and was arrested as a Christian during the time of Diocletian. He called upon God during his trials and through God's power he survived tortures. At one point, George called down fires from Heaven to consume his pagan persecutors.

$\mathcal{A}$PRIL

4th Sunday (4-4)

St. Mark, Evangelist *(April 25th)*
ALIVE CIRCA 10-70 AD

Boucicaut Master, *Mark Cutting a Pen,* c. 1420
FRENCH INTERNATIONAL STYLE

Located at the Pierpont Morgan Library, New York

$\mathcal{M}$ARK WAS THE AUTHOR of the gospel that bears his name. Little is known about him save that he was Bishop of Alexandria. St. Paul writes of Mark during his captivities when Mark served St. Paul and was a help to him. It is also believed he was a close friend of St. Peter and active in Rome, but there is no historical evidence to support this.

$\mathcal{A}$PRIL

5th Sunday (4-5)

St. Philip Apostle *(May 1st)*

Peter Paul Rubens, *St Philip*, 1610-1612
FLEMISH BAROQUE

Located at the Museo Nacional del Prado

INITIALLY UNDER THE INFLUENCE of St. John the Baptist, Philip was called to Christ following Peter and Andrew. However, little is known of him except for his appearances in the Gospels; an example is the feeding of the five thousand *(John 6.5-6.8)*. Eusebius writes that Philip preached the gospel before his death.

$\mathcal{M}$AY

1st Sunday (5-1)

St. James the Younger *(May 1st)*
DIED C. 62 AD

El Greco, *St. James the Younger,* 1510-1514
SPANISH RENAISSANCE

*Two versions, this one is located at the Museo de El Greco, Toledo
(another is at the Art Institute of Chicago)*

ACCORDING TO EUSEBIUS, a historian of the Church from the third and fourth centuries, James the younger was the Bishop of Jerusalem *(Galatians 1.10-24).* In Galatians, Paul also refers to James as "the Lord's Brother," which marks this James as the one mentioned in the Gospel of Mark as the brother of Jesus *(Mark 6.3).* This James is also widely accepted as the author of the Epistle of James, which promotes good works as an expression of faith.

$\mathcal{M}$AY

2nd Sunday (5-2)

Mother's Day *(2nd Sunday of May)*

Sandro Botticelli, *The Adoration of the Child*, c. 1500
ITALIAN RENAISSANCE

Located at the North Carolina Museum of Art, Raleigh

WITHIN THE BIBLE, Mary is portrayed as a saintly paragon of motherhood. She tenderly cares for the young child and with great strength maintains her composure despite the knowledge she has of her son's bleak, earthly future. Even at His death, Mary is present watching as Jesus suffers for mankind *(Mark 15.40)*.

$\mathcal{M}$AY

3rd Sunday (5-3)

The Sacrifice of Isaac
GENESIS 22.1-14

Rembrandt, *The Sacrifice of Isaac,* 1635
DUTCH BAROQUE

Alte Pinakothek, Munich

GOD SAID TO ABRAHAM, "Take your son, your only son Isaac, who you love, and go to the land of Moriah, and offer him there as a burnt offering on one of the mountains that I shall show you" *(Genesis 22.2).* Having heard the command of the Lord, Abraham proceeded to the mountains in the land of Moriah and prepared to make his only son a sacrifice to demonstrate his faith in the Lord. Yet the Lord saw that Abraham was faithful, and so an angel stayed his hand *(Genesis 22.10-14)* and a ram was provided in the place of his son. Like God's offering of His Son, Jesus Christ for Christians, here, too, Abraham sought to sacrifice his only son as an offering of his faith.

$\mathcal{M}$AY

4th Sunday

St. Bede the Venerable *(May 27th)*

B. 672 D. 735

Unknown Mosaic Master, *St. Bede,* 15th century

Located at Westminster Cathedral, London

*B*EDE IS THE ONLY ENGLISH SAINT to be included in Dante's Paradisio in *The Divine Comedy;* this is indicative of his importance in the early English Church. He wrote *The Ecclesiastical History of the English People,* which is still read today. He also translated many Latin and Greek texts into English, thereby making available classical and ecclesiastical learning to the newly converted of England. Many of his original manuscripts still survive.

$\mathcal{M}$AY

5th Sunday (5-5)

The Visitation *(May 31st)*
LUKE 1.39-56

Jacopo Pontormo, *The Visitation*, 1528-1529
ITALIAN MANNERISM

Located at San Michele, Carmignano, Florence

SHORTLY AFTER THE ANNUNCIATION *(Luke 1.26-38)*, Mary sets out to a small town in Judea where the house of Zechariah and Elizabeth is located. When Mary had greeted Elizabeth, "the child [John the Baptist] leaped in her womb" *(Luke 1.41)*, and Elizabeth understandingly, said to Mary, "Blessed are you among women, and blessed is the fruit of your womb" *(Luke 1.42)*. And so John the Baptist met the earthly mother of the Blessed One, whom he would later baptize in the Jordan, before his own birth.

*J*UNE

1st Sunday (6-1)

St. Columba *(June 9th)*
B. 521 D. 597

MS. Rawl, *St Columba,* c. 16th century
MEDIEVAL MANUSCRIPT

Located at the Bodleian Library, Oxford University

*A*FTER STUDYING IN VARIOUS MONASTERIES and becoming an ordained priest, Columba went throughout Ireland preaching to the pagans and establishing monasteries along the way. After a bloody battle between rival clans, for which Columba took responsibility, he exiled himself from Ireland with a planned penance: to gather as many souls as possible. He Christianized Iona, an island near Ireland, and then turned his missionary attentions to the Scottish Picts. In one of his ascribed miracles, Columba mysteriously opened the gates of a pagan castle through the intervention of God. His memory is still held dear by the Scottish churches.

*J*UNE

2nd Sunday (6-2)

Pentecost *(50 days after Easter)*
ACTS 2.1-41

Jean Restout, *Pentecost,* 1732
FRENCH LATE-BAROQUE

Located at the Musee de Louvre, Paris

*F*IFTY DAYS AFTER EASTER (and in the Jewish tradition fifty days after Passover), the apostles were gathered and the Holy Spirit descended upon them.

And suddenly from heaven there came a sound like the rush of a violent wind, and it filled the entire house where they were sitting... All of them were filled with the Holy Spirit and began to speak in other languages, as the spirit gave them ability *(Acts 2.2-4)*.

As a result of this miracle, several devout Jews were converted and baptized, thereby establishing a tradition of Baptism on Pentecost *(Acts 2.41)*.

$\mathcal{J}$UNE

3rd Sunday (6-3)

Father's Day (3rd Sunday of June)
LUKE 15.11-32

Rembrandt, *The Return of the Prodigal Son,* 1689
DUTCH BAROQUE

Located at the Hermitage, St. Petersburg

"For this son of mine was dead and is alive again; he was lost and is found!"
(Luke 15.24).

I N ONE OF JESUS' PARABLES, He tells of a man whose son asks for his inheritance early and then wastefully spends it. When a famine comes, the son suffers since he has squandered his fortune, and so he returns to his father in order to ask for work. After hearing his son, the father mercifully accepts his son as if he had never squandered his fortune or done anything wrong.

JUNE

4th Sunday (6-4)

St. Peter *(June 29th)*

Rembrandt, *Peter Denying Christ*, 1660
DUTCH BAROQUE

Located at the Rijksmuseum, Amsterdam

"Truly I tell you, this very night, before the cock crows, you will deny me three times" *(Matthew 26.34).*

IF THERE CAN BE SAID to be a leader of the apostles, then it was certainly Simon Peter. His prominence in all four of the Gospels and in *Acts* marks him as such. In Pentecost, for instance, Peter plays the principal role of Baptizer *(Acts 2.38-41).* He is also the Apostle upon whom Christ states He will build His church *(Matthew 16.18-20),* so Peter is often thought of as the first pope or patriarch of the church. Peter performed many miracles after the death of Christ. The site of his tomb is St. Peter's Basilica in Rome.

$\mathcal{J}$UNE

5th Sunday (6-5)

The Martyrdom of St. Paul *(June 29th)*

Tintoretto, *The Martyrdom of St. Paul,* 1556
ITALIAN MANNERISM

Located at the Madonna Dell'orto, Venice

"And turning toward the east, Paul lifted up his hands to heaven and prayed at length; and after having conversed in Hebrew with the fathers during prayer he bent his neck, without speaking anymore" *(Acts of Paul 6)*.

$\mathcal{T}$HE MARTYRDOM OF ST. PAUL is not told in any of the canonical books of the Bible. It instead survives as an apocryphal tale titled the *Acts of Paul.* The historical Paul is believed to have been killed around the year 60, when he was beheaded instead of being crucified because of his status as a Roman citizen. It is said that when his head was lopped off, milk splashed from his neck, and the centurion who executed him was converted by the sight of this miracle.

*J*ULY

1st Sunday (7-1)

Isaiah, Old Testament prophet *(July 6th)*

Giovanni Battista Tiepolo, *The Prophet Isaiah*, 1726–1729
ITALIAN LATE-BAROQUE

Located at the Palazzo Patriarcale, Udine

*I*SAIAH IS GENERALLY CONSIDERED the preeminent prophet for Christianity. Jerome, for instance, considered him to be more of an evangelist than a prophet because of his ability to reveal the mysteries of the Church. Throughout his eponymous book, Isaiah considers how God involves himself in the affairs of the world as he watched an Assyrian army assault the Kingdom of Judah.

"Zion shall be redeemed by justice, and those in her who repent, by righteousness. But rebels and sinners shall be destroyed together, and those who forsake the lord shall be consumed" *(Isaiah 1.27-28).*

ʝULY

2nd Sunday (7-2)

Ezekiel, Old Testament prophet *(July 21st)*

Raphael, *The Vision of Ezekiel,* 1518
ITALIAN, FLORENTINE RENAISSANCE

Located at the Galleria Palatina, Florence

THE LAST OF THE THREE MAJOR PROPHETS, Ezekiel was a Zadokite priest who exiled himself in Babylonia. His writings date from just after the Babylonians destroyed Jerusalem and the Temple in 586 BC. This event challenged the traditional belief that God had chosen Zion as the holy city and its citizens as the holy people. Ultimately, he determines that it is the wicked ways of the Jews that have caused the Lord's grace to depart.

"Then the glory of the Lord rose up from the cherub to the threshold of the house … And the glory of the lord ascended from the middle of the city, and stopped on the mountain east of the city" *(Isaiah 10.1-22 and 11.22-25).*

$\mathcal{J}$ULY

3rd Sunday (7-3)

St. Mary Magdalene *(July 22nd)*

Titian, *Penitent Mary Magdalene,* 1565
ITALIAN, VENETIAN RENAISSANCE

Located at the Hermitage, St. Petersburg

"Do not be afraid, for I know that you seek Jesus who was crucified. He is not here, for he is risen" *(Matthew 28.5-6).*

$\mathcal{M}$ARY MAGDALENE WAS formerly possessed by demons, but became a follower of Jesus *(Luke 8.2).* She was present when the angel appeared to the Marys at the tomb and was also the first person to see the newly-resurrected Christ. As such, Mary Magdalene is accorded respect and honor throughout the Christian tradition, and her salvation has come to symbolically represent the possibility of salvation through Christ.

$\mathcal{J}$ULY

4th Sunday (7-4)

St. James the Elder *(July 25th)*

Giovanni Battista Tiepolo, *St. James the Greater*
Conquering the Moors, 1749-1750
ITALIAN LATE-BAROQUE

Located at the Szépmûvészeti Múzeum, Budapest

ST. JAMES THE ELDER (OR GREATER) was the brother of St. John the Evangelist and one of the three Apostles present at the Transfiguration. After the death of Christ, he is believed to have gone to Spain. In 812, the tomb of St. James was discovered and after the Vatican's confirmation, the tomb became a vital pilgrimage site. Throughout the Middle Ages, James's tomb became one of the most important pilgrimage sites. Santiago de Compostela was constructed over his tomb. It is also believed by the Spanish that James's assisted them in fending off the Moors who constantly attacked Spain.

*J*ULY

5th Sunday (7-5)

St. Martha *(July 29th)*

Tintoretto, *Christ in the House of Mary and Martha,* c. 1580
ITALIAN MANNERISM

Located at the Alte Pinakothek, Munich

*M*ARTHA WAS THE SISTER OF MARY and Lazarus, both of whom played principal parts in the New Testament. When Christ came to her, and she begged him to get Mary to help her with the house work, Christ said "Martha, Martha, you are worried and distracted by many things; there is need of only one thing. Mary has chosen the better part, which will not be taken away from her" *(Luke 10.40-42).* And so like her sister, Martha became a devoted and faithful servant of the Lord.

$\mathcal{A}$UGUST

1st Sunday (8-1)

St. Lawrence *(July 10th)*

Titian, *The Martyrdom of St. Laurence,* 1548-1559
ITALIAN, VENETIAN RENAISSANCE

Located at the Church of the Gesuiti, Venice

LITTLE IS KNOWN OF LAWRENCE except when and why he died. In 257 the Emperor Valerian made edicts against the Christians and the current Pope, St. Sixtus. The many traditions portray St. Lawrence as a faithful and obedient martyr for God who followed his pope to death. In one particular version a Roman prefect demands tribute from Lawrence and the Christian community, and so Lawrence promises to bring him the riches of the Church. When he brings Christ's followers before the prefect, the prefect has Lawrence burnt slowly upon a grid-iron because of his failure to bring gold.

Augs

2nd Sunday (8-2)

The Fiery Furnace
DANIEL 1, 2, 3

Anon., *The Fiery Furnace*, c. 4th century
EARLY CHRISTIAN

Located at the Priscilla Catacombs, Rome

SHADRACH, MESHACH, AND ABEDNEGO were three servants of Judea who were trained in the arts of the Babylonian court. When King Nebuchadnezzar built a golden statue and demanded the submission of everyone, the three aforementioned men were "thrown into a furnace of blazing fire" for their failure to renounce their God and worship the idol *(Daniel 3.11)*. Having thrown them into the fire, the King said, "Was it not three men that we threw bound into the fire ... But I see four men unbound, walking in the middle of the fire, and they are not hurt" *(Daniel 3.24-25)*. Then, with heavenly help, the three men were saved from the fire. Recognizing the power of their faith, Nebuchadnezzar made a decree protecting the God and faith of Shadrach, Meshach, and Abednego.

$\mathcal{A}$UGUST

3rd Sunday (8-3)

St. Bartholomew *(August 24th)*

Giovanni Battista Tiepolo, *The Martyrdom of St. Bartholomew,*
1722
ITALIAN LATE-BAROQUE

Located at the San Stae, Venice

LIKE MANY OF THE APOSTLES, details concerning Bartholomew are elusive. Yet the popular traditions provide a fuller picture of his life. Bartholomew is said to have preached in India (here meaning Persia, Arabia, and Northern Africa) and Greater Armenia. After he converted many souls for Christ, the barbarians of those lands flayed him alive and then beheaded him.

$\mathcal{A}$UGUST

4th Sunday (8-4)

St. Augustine of Hippo *(August 28th)*

Fillipino Lippi, *St. Augustine,* c. 1490
EARLY ITALIAN RENAISSANCE

Located at the North Carolina Museum of Art, Raleigh.
Gift of the Samuel H. Kress Foundation

AUGUSTINE IS PROBABLY BEST KNOWN for two famous written works *Confessions* and *City of God.* In the former, Augustine attempted to reveal all of his shortcomings and failures; in the latter, he sought to refute the blasphemy of the Alaric Goths who sacked Rome in 410. Augustine served as Bishop of Hippo and generally sought to cleanse the church of all scandal and wrongdoing, and his writings demonstrate that he began this cleansing with himself. Accordingly, he was awarded the title "Doctor of the Church" after his death.

$\mathcal{A}$UGUST

5th Sunday

The Martyrdom of St. John the Baptist *(August 29th)*

Unknown Master, *The Martyrdom of St. John the Baptist,* 1350
ITALIAN MIDDLE AGES

Located at the Basilica di San Marco, Venice

JESUS STATES THAT JOHN THE BAPTIST fulfills the Old Testament prophecy of the return of Elijah *(Matthew 17.10),* which is necessary for Christ's validation as the Messiah. After John criticized Herod for divorcing his wife, Herod had John imprisoned. On Herod's birthday, Salome danced for him, and he granted her request: "Give me the head of John the Baptist here on a platter" *(Matthew 14.8).* Herod had John beheaded, and the head was presented to Salome on a platter.

SEPTEMBER

1st Sunday (9-1)

Jonah, Old Testament Prophet *(September 22nd)*

Michelangelo, *Jonah*, 1511
ITALIAN, FLORENTINE RENAISSANCE

Located at the Sistine Chapel, Rome

THE BOOK OF JONAH differs from the books of prophecy. It is a narrative of Jonah, rather than a collection of prophecies. Jonah is called by God and tries to escape his calling. He could not do so and is captured by a large fish: "But the Lord provided a large fish to swallow up Jonah; and Jonah was in the belly of the fish three days and three nights" *(Jonah 1.17)*. Jonah submitted to God's will and did His bidding. This narrative is cast by most theologians as a prototype for the Resurrection of Christ in the New Testament.

SEPTEMBER

2nd Sunday (9-2)

Holy Cross Day *(September 14th)*

Cimabue, *Crucifix,* 1268-1271
ITALIAN LATE-MIDDLE AGES/PROTO-RENAISSANCE

Located at the Church of San Domenico, Arezzo

WHEREAS GOOD FRIDAY is a celebration of Christ's passion and his sacrifice for mankind, Holy Cross Day celebrates the cross as the physical instrument of salvation. The origin of cross veneration can be traced to the narratives surrounding Helena (c. fourth century) and the finding of the true cross, the most famous version coming from The Golden Legend. A cross like this one would have been hung above the altar of a church.

SEPTEMBER

3rd Sunday (9-3)

St. Matthew, Apostle *(September 21st)*

Caravaggio, *The Calling of St. Matthew*, 1599-1600
ITALIAN BAROQUE

Located at the Contarelli Chapel, San Luigi dei Francesci, Rome

"As Jesus was walking along, he saw a man called Matthew sitting at the tax booth; and he said to him, 'Follow me.' And he got up and followed him" *(Matthew 9.9)*.

MATTHEW WAS A TAX COLLECTOR, a profession that was nearly universally hated by the people of the Roman Empire. Matthew directed his Gospel toward the Jews. He also preached throughout the ancient world, spreading the Word of the Lord.

September

4th Sunday (9-4)

Ss. Cosmas and Damian, Martyrs *(September 27th)*
D. 287

Fra Angelico, *The Crucifixion of SS. Cosmas and Damian,*
1438-1440
ITALIAN EARLY-RENAISSANCE

Located at the Alte Pinakothek, Munich

COSMAS AND DAMIAN WERE twin brothers who practiced medicine out of charity rather than for fees. They were also enthusiastic missionaries for the Christian faith in a dangerous time. During the reign of Diocletian, Cosmas and Damian were arrested, tormented, and then finally killed by Lysias of Cilicia.

SEPTEMBER

5th Sunday (9-5)

St. Jerome *(September 30th)*
B. 342 D. 420

Giovanni Bellini, *St. Jerome Reading in the Countryside,* 1480-1490
ITALIAN, VENETIAN RENAISSANCE

Located at the National Gallery of Art, Washington, D.C.

EROME WAS MOST LEARNED in the Scriptures; a master of Latin, Greek, and Hebrew; and a translator of the Old Testament from Hebrew into Greek and Latin. His commentary on the Scriptures is perhaps his most valued contribution, and for this he was given the title "Doctor of the Church." His understanding of the scriptures also allowed him to defend Christianity from attacks by heretics and blasphemers. He is also one of the Desert Fathers whose work led to the development of monastic orders.

OCTOBER

1st Sunday (10-1)

St. Francis of Assisi *(October 4th)*
B. 1182 D. 1226

Giovanni Bellini, *St. Francis in Ecstasy,* 1480-1485
ITALIAN, VENETIAN RENAISSANCE

Located at the Frick Collection, New York

ST. FRANCIS WAS BORN IN ASSISI to a wealthy family. Before his calling, Francis was a man who gave with charity to the needy and helped those he could by his worldly means. One day while he was praying in a small, old church, God spoke to him and said, "Go and repair my house, which you see is falling down." So he sought to repair the small church where he was praying. His father grew angry with Francis's project and disinherited him, and as a result Francis relinquished worldly things. He went on to form the Franciscan order of monks and also received the Stigmata.

OCTOBER

2nd Sunday (10-2)

Abraham, Patriarch *(October 9th)*

Gerbrand Van Den Eeckhout, *Abraham and the Three Angels,* 1658
DUTCH BAROQUE

Located at the Hermitage, St. Petersburg

BRAHAM, A DESCENDANT OF NOAH, was called by God to leave his home and allow God to guide him to a new land. In *Genesis 15.1-21,* God made a covenant with Abraham and promised him a multitude of descendents. In the scene depicted here, three angels appeared to Abraham as men, and he accepted them with hospitality. It was also during this scene that one of the angels announced to Abraham that he will be given a son by his barren wife Sarah, to which Sarah responds by laughing *(Genesis 18.1-15).*

OCTOBER

3rd Sunday (10-3)

St. Luke, Apostle *(October 18th)*

Rogier Van Der Weyden, *St. Luke Drawing a Portrait of the Madonna,* 1435
NORTHERN TRADITION

Located at the Museum of Fine Arts, Boston

LUKE IS ONE OF THE FOUR EVANGELISTS, who prior to conversion to Christianity was a physician working in the region of Antioch. Luke became a follower of Paul and was his helper until his martyrdom. Besides writing one of the Synoptic Gospels, Luke is believed to have been an artist and the first icon painter of the Christian tradition. Luke also wrote the Acts of the Apostles.

OCTOBER

4th Sunday (10-4)

Reformation Day *(October 31st)*

Lucas Cranach the Elder, *Portrait of Martin Luther,* 1543
NORTHERN TRADITION

Located at Germanisches National Museum, Nuremberg

IN 1516, A DOMINICAN FRIAR was sent to Germany in order to collect indulgences as funding for the new St. Peter's Basilica in Rome. On October 31, 1517, Martin Luther protested the selling of indulgences by posting the *Ninety-Five Theses.* For Luther, the selling of indulgences could not absolve a sinner's sin; that is God's prerogative alone. Thus the Reformation was set in motion.

1535

OCTOBER

5th Sunday (10-5)

St. Simon, Apostle *(October 28th)*

Peter Paul Rubens, *St. Simon,* 1610-1612
FLEMISH BAROQUE

Located at the Museo del Prado, Madrid

LITTLE IS KNOWN ABOUT St. Simon the Zealot. It is known that he fastidiously studied Jewish law before his calling. According to Roman tradition, he is believed to have preached in Egypt where he joined St. Jude. Together they went and preached in Persia and both eventually were martyred.

NOVEMBER

1st Sunday (11-1)

All Saints Day *(November 1st)*

Jan van Eyck, *Adoration of the Lamb,* 1425-1429
NORTHERN TRADITION
NOTE: *This is a predella from the Ghent Altarpiece.*

Located at the Cathedral of St. Bavo, Ghent

ALL SAINTS DAY, or All Hallows day, is a celebration of all saints who have gone to heaven.

NOVEMBER

2nd Sunday (11-2)

St. Martin of Tours *(November 11th)*
B. 316 D. 397

Anthony van Dyck, *St. Martin Dividing his Cloak,* 1618
FLEMISH BAROQUE

Located at the Church of St. Martin, Zaventem

ST. MARTIN WAS BORN IN SABARIA, now Hungary, and he became a soldier before he was called to Christ. While in the military, Martin, seeing a beggar that his company was passing by, divided his cloak so that the beggar might be clothed. While asleep that very night, Christ appeared to Martin stating that He Himself had been clothed by Martin. During a barbarian invasion around this time, Martin left the army in order to become a soldier for Christ. For the remainder of his life he defended the faith from attacks by heretics and blasphemers. His tomb became an important pilgrimage site at Tours where he was bishop when he died.

November

3rd Sunday (11-3)

St. Elizabeth of Hungary *(November 17th)*
B.1207 D. 1231

Unknown Master, *Elizabeth Giving Bread and Wine to Beggars,*
1515
Northern Tradition

Located at the Fundación Colección Thyssen-Bornemisza, Pedralbes

Elizabeth was a thirteenth-century princess of the Magyar Kingdom (Hungary) who was married at age fourteen. When she was widowed at age twenty, she relinquished her wealth and distributed it to the less fortunate. Because of her charity she became a symbol of Christian grace in the Church immediately after her death in 1231 (maybe from the plague).

$\mathcal{N}$OVEMBER

4th Sunday (11-4)

Thanksgiving *(4th Thursday of November)*

Giovanni Battista Tiepolo, *The Last Supper,* 1745-1747
ITALIAN LATE-BAROQUE

Located at the Musee de Louvre, Paris

$\mathcal{F}$OR AMERICANS, the tradition of Thanksgiving can be traced to a celebration in 1621 at Plymouth. The first Thanksgiving was a feast held to honor the food received from the local Native Americans in a time of need. This event can be related to the spiritual meal which Christ instituted with the Last Supper.

Ɲovember

5th Sunday (11-5)

St. Andrew *(November 30th)*

Duccio, *The Calling of Peter and Andrew,* 1308-1311
ITALIAN LATE-GOTHIC, PROTO-RENAISSANCE
NOTE: *Reverse Predella from the Maesta*

Located at the National Gallery of Art, Washington, D.C.

ANDREW, BROTHER TO SIMON PETER, was a disciple of St. John the Baptist and witnessed John proclaim the following about Jesus Christ: "Here is the lamb of God who takes away the sin of the world" *(John 1.29)*. From then on Andrew followed Christ, realizing He was the Messiah. After Christ's death, Andrew went about preaching and converting. He suffered martyrdom on an X-shaped cross, called a saltire, from which he preached for two days before succumbing to death.

$\mathcal{D}$ECEMBER

1st Sunday (12-1)

St. Barbara *(December 4th)*
C. 3RD CENTURY

Ghirlandaio, *St. Barbara Crushing her Infidel Father,* 1471
ITALIAN, FLORENTINE RENAISSANCE

Located at the Parish Church of Sant'Andrea, Cercina

IN THE TIME OF MAXIMIAN'S REIGN there was a rich pagan named Dioscorus. He had a young daughter named Barbara whom he kept guarded within a tower. Barbara was a devout Christian according to the early writers, and she even installed three windows in her bathhouse to symbolize the Trinity. Her father was enraged when he discovered her faith and eventually she was brought before a judge. After she had been put through tortures and refused to renounce her faith, she was executed as a Roman citizen by decapitation.

DECEMBER

2nd Sunday (12-2)

St. Lucy *(December 13th)*
B. 283 D. 304

Lorenzo Lotto, *St. Lucy Before the Judge,* 1532
ITALIAN RENAISSANCE

Located at the Pinacoteca Civica, Iesi

ACCORDING TO LEGEND, Lucy was a resident of Syracuse, who having been pushed towards marriage by her parents, gave herself and her virginity up to the Lord. She kept her pact with God a secret. However, her suitor eventually discovered this and became enraged. He accused her of being a Christian in front of a judge during the height of Diocletian's persecutions, and she was subsequently killed with a sword through the neck.

DECEMBER

3rd Sunday (12-3)

St. Thomas, Apostle *(December 21st)*

Marten de Vos, *St. Thomas Altarpiece,* 1574
DUTCH RENAISSANCE

Located at the Koninklijk Museum voor Shone Kunsten, Antwerp

"Have you believed because you have seen me? Blessed are those who have not seen and yet have come to believe" *(John 20.29).*

THOMAS, ONE OF THE TWELVE APOSTLES, was not present when Jesus appeared following the Resurrection. Thomas doubted if Christ had truly risen, and he said "Unless I see the mark of the nails in his hands and put my finger in the mark of the nails and my hand in his side, I will not believe." *(John 20.25).* A week after this Christ reappeared to the Apostles. He said to Thomas, "Put your finger here and see my hands. Reach out your hand and put in my side. Do not doubt but believe" *(John 20.27).* Thomas doubted no longer. After the Ascension of Christ, Thomas turned to missionary work and ultimately was martyred.

DECEMBER

4th Sunday (12-4)

Christmas *(December 25th)*

Ghirlandaio, *Adoration of the Shepherds,* 1483-1485
ITALIAN, FLORENTINE RENAISSANCE

Located at Santa Trinita, Florence

"Do not be afraid; for see — I am bringing you good news of great joy for all people: to you is born this day in the city of David a Savior, who is the Messiah, the Lord" *(Luke 2.10-11).*

IN THE TOWN of Bethlehem Christ was born as the Savior for mankind, the Messiah.

DECEMBER

5th Sunday (12-5)

St. Stephen, the First Martyr *(December 26th)*

Pietro da Cortona, *The Stoning of St. Stephen,* c. 1660
ITALIAN BAROQUE

Located at the Hermitage, St. Petersburg

STEPHEN, ONE OF THE CHOSEN seven in *Acts 6*, became a deacon of the Christian Church. It is said that those who argued against Stephen "could not withstand the wisdom and the Spirit with which he spoke" *(Acts 6.10)*. When arguing against certain people of the temple who accused him of attempting to destroy the law, he said to them, "You stiff-necked people, uncircumcised in heart and ears … You are the ones that received the law as ordained by angels, and yet you have not kept it" *(Acts 7.51-53)*. This enraged the Jews and "Then they dragged him out of the city and began to stone him" *(Acts 7.58)*. Thus, Stephen became the first martyr for the Christian faith.

Movable Feasts

Palm Sunday (One Sunday prior to Easter)

The Entry into Jerusalem *(M-1)*
MARK 11.1-11; MATTHEW 21.1-9; LUKE 19.28-38; JOHN 12.12-15

Giotto, *Entry into Jerusalem,* 1304-1306
ITALIAN LATE-GOTHIC, PROTO-RENAISSANCE

Located at the Scrovegni Chapel (the Arena Chapel), Padua

*F*ULFILLING ZECHERIAH'S PROPHECY *(Zecheriah 9.9-10),* Christ arrived triumphantly at Jerusalem. His procession seems to have led the Romans to compare this event to that of a Roman emperor entering a city following a victory. His entry into the city marks the beginning of Holy Week.

Movable Feasts

Good Friday (The Friday before Easter)

The Crucifixion and Death of Christ *(M-2)*
Mark 15.16-39; Matthew 27.27-48; Luke 23.18-43; John 19.17-30

Rogier Van Der Weyden, *Descent from the Cross,* 1435
Northern Tradition

Located at the Museo del Prado, Madrid

And so, following the betrayal in the garden of Gethsemane *(Luke 22.31-53),* Christ was tried as a usurper of authority and executed according to Roman fashion. His cross was placed on Golgotha (the place of the skull), on His head was placed the crown of thorns, and written on His cross was "King of the Jews." Christ gave His mortal body to God as a sacrifice for humankind, as penance for their sins, and He granted to mankind redemption and salvation.

Movable Feasts

Easter Sunday

The Resurrection of Jesus Christ *(M-3)*

Fra Angelico, *Noli Me Tangere,* 1440-1442
ITALIAN, EARLY RENAISSANCE

Located at the Convento di San Marco, Florence

"Why do you look for the living among the dead? He is not here, but has risen" *(Luke 24.5)*.

DURING THE INTERMEDIATE TIME between Christ's burial and the coming of the women to the tomb, Christ rose from the dead and walked again amongst the living. His triumphant victory over death demonstrates how faith in God will allow mankind to vanquish death and live an everlasting existence in communion with God. For Christ died in order to abolish death.

$\mathcal{M}$OVABLE $\mathcal{F}$EASTS

Ascension Day (40 Days after Easter)

The Ascension of Jesus Christ *(M-4)*

Rembrandt, *Ascension of Christ,* 1636
DUTCH BAROQUE

Located at the Alte Pinakothek, Munich

"Then he led them [the apostles] out as far as Bethany, and, lifting up his hands, he blessed them. While he was blessing them, he withdrew from them and was carried up into heaven" *(Luke 24.50-51).*

FORTY DAYS AFTER HIS RESURRECTION, on Easter Christ ascended back into heaven to sit at the right hand of God.

General Index

B

F

G

I

J

K

M

S

T

Biblical Index

John

Index to Works of Art